LIFE AFTER COLLEGE

What to expect and how to succeed in your career

ANDY MASTERS

First Edition

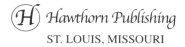 Hawthorn Publishing
ST. LOUIS, MISSOURI

LIFE AFTER COLLEGE
What to expect and how to succeed in your career

by Andy Masters

Published by:
Hawthorn Publishing
Post Office Box 1167
St. Louis, MO 63022-1167

Printed in the United States of America
9 8 7 6 5 4 3 2 1

Library of Congress Control Number: 2004113621
ISBN 0-9754-6103-6
Masters, Andy
Life After College: What to expect and how to succeed in your career / Andy Masters.—1st ed.

LIFE AFTER COLLEGE

What to expect and how to succeed in your career

Andy Masters

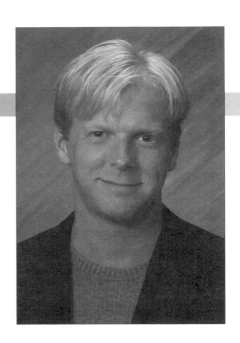

Andy Masters

Andy Masters took full advantage of his college experience throughout undergraduate school. He served as Student Government Association President at the University of Missouri-St. Louis, and was honored as "Greek Man of the Year," representing Sigma Tau Gamma Fraternity. Andy later achieved Distinguished Graduate honors at Webster University, attending evening graduate school while engineering his daytime career.

B.A. - Communications, 1994, University of Missouri-St. Louis
B.A. - Political Science, 1994, University of Missouri-St. Louis
M.A. - Human Resources Development, 1997, Webster University
M.A. - Marketing, 2000, Webster University

Andy has gained extensive experience in sales, marketing, and management across several industries, and is now president of his own training and consulting firm. Andy actively speaks to college students who search for direction, advice, resources, and inspiration. He is also a member of the Association for the Promotion of Campus Activities (APCA).

To inquire about Andy's *Life After College*™ on-campus program, or other consulting, training, or speaking opportunities for your university or organization, contact Masters Performance Improvement at 1-888-MPI-SELL (1-888-674-7355), or visit:

www.life-after-college.com

To my parents, Charles and Ann.
I never even would have made it to college,
let alone graduated,
if it wasn't for their support and encouragement
along the way.

Contents

Chapter Five: Simon Says "Follow the Rules" 85

Chapter Six: Formal Advice for Informal Situations 99

Chapter Seven: Spectacular Career Development 115

Chapter Eight: Planning Your Ultimate Road to Success 133

Index 153

Acknowledgments

I would like to thank Matt Ronken, Christine Ronken, Michael Quinn, and Lisa Schoenherr for their valuable content review and contribution. I would also like to thank Sue Sylvia for her fabulous book design, and Michael Tolle for his meticulous copyediting. Much appreciation goes to Tamara Gegg-LaPlume at Webster University Career Services, and Allyson Wilson at the University of Missouri-St. Louis Office of Student Life.

Preface

The purpose of this book, as well as my on-campus speaking program *Life After College*™, is to provide direction, advice, resources, and inspiration to those just entering, or soon to enter the workforce. I want to help the reader—YOU—be ahead of the game from the outset of your career. If you read this book, and practice its principles, I strongly believe you will be.

I was fortunate enough to gain a tremendous amount of knowledge, experience, and assistance through Sigma Tau Gamma Fraternity, Student Government Association, alumni groups, friends, and most importantly parents. They provided support, mentoring, professional contacts, and resources for which I will be forever grateful.

Yet, even with such a head start these groups provided, there is still so much more preparation you need for what you are about to encounter. Thus, half of this book is devoted to things I exercised during my first 10 years after college. The other half covers things I wish I had known.

"If I only knew then what I know now."

This book contains valuable resources you can refer to for more information in specific areas. Such resources include books, magazines, websites, organizations, seminars, and more. Keep this book as a handy reference for any particular challenges or areas of development you may have along the way. This book also contains many clichés and colloquial expressions common in the business world today that you should become accustomed to hearing. There is wisdom and purpose in their meaning, so I encourage you to ponder them.

Lack of preparation for this transition from the college environment to the working world can lead to a major culture shock. The contents of this book, including all of its recommended resources, provide valuable advice and information critical for this transition. Without such preparation, many graduates may make poor decisions early in their career track, waste several misguided years spinning their wheels, or make professional mistakes that cause irreparable damage. There are many lessons that can be learned more easily now, as opposed to being learned "the hard way" later.

There is another motivation for writing this book. I feel there is a tremendous void of knowledge for young adults who are in the stage between graduating college and entering the workforce. There are critical rites of passage that are not taught in the college classroom, and are certainly not taught in books on how to write a resume and how to perform in an interview. Such books overwhelm the shelves at university bookstores.

Yet, too often, graduating seniors fall into the trap of just trying to "get a job." This decision will have a tremendous impact on the rest of their lives. There are many important things to consider. This book will help answer questions such as:

"What is really important to me in selecting a career?"
"OK, I've got a job....now what?"
"What does it take to be successful in my first 10 years?"

Hopefully, this book will help you consider your life and career goals, and help you achieve them. I have learned and experienced a tremendous amount during my 10 years since undergraduate school. And my graduate degrees in human resources development and marketing are the perfect combination needed to provide career advice and self-promotion strategies to those who seek it. Therefore, I want to serve as a mentor to every reader. Everyone needs mentors.

Mentoring demands that you tell people not only the things they want to hear, but also the things they don't necessarily want to hear—but need to hear. Mentoring also calls for you to challenge people. I hope this book will challenge you, as well.

Chapter One:

Know What You Want and What You Value

Five Words Of Advice...

…for those who are still college students…

"Enjoy It While You Can!"

Those grueling days of going to class from 9:00 a.m. – 11:45 a.m. are almost over. Retirement from college academics is near, with a whole lifetime filled with study complete. Your hard work is about ready to pay off. Easy street is next, right?

Think again!

Unfortunately, life is tough. Most graduates will begin working 40 hours per week *at a minimum* in the real world. This includes getting up early *every day*, challenging traffic both to and from work, and spending the majority of your waking hours with co-workers, not friends or family. You could be an early candidate for "post-party" depression.

What you do have to look forward to is molding a career from scratch that only you will control. Your career can be enjoyable, challenging, rewarding, and hopefully prosperous.

It's never too late to continue building your resume before you graduate. Keep pushing, and finish your college career strong. Strive to graduate with the best GPA you can earn. Try to win awards, earn certifications, and gain any other tangible skills you can. This may include computer/technical skills, communication/public speaking skills, or fluency in a second language.

You won't find a more outspoken proponent for extra-curricular activities and college organizations than me. They help build character, responsibility, social skills, and leadership skills that can last you a life-time. A resume that includes a degree and extra-curricular activities looks much stronger than a resume with just a degree. Get involved by holding offices and making contributions within those campus organizations. Certainly, I owe so much to such organizations that were key to my personal development. Since undergraduate school, I have continued to gain friends, professional contacts, and many other resources by such involvement.

Many professional organizations welcome membership by collegians, as well. Both the American Marketing Association and American Management Association (AMA and AMA, respectively) are such examples. What a great way to make contacts and learn from mentors before you even enter the profession. You can also receive their publica-tions and e-mail updates to keep up with industry trends and current events. Consider joining a professional organization related to your field between now and the day you graduate, if you haven't already.

Try to schedule a lunch or meeting with someone who may be in the field you think you want to enter. If you don't know of anyone, seek out your career center, university alumni association, or professors who have plenty of contacts in the field. Obtaining valuable feedback from those who have been down your path before may help you avoid mistakes and focus your objectives.

No matter what point you are at in your college career, you should always be trying to keep career planning on the forefront of your mind. Don't wait until the second semester of your senior year to begin thinking about it. Research industry trends and salary surveys now, and continue to expand your skills and knowledge in addition to just pursuing your degree.

"Today is the first day of the rest of your life."
                                                    - Charles Dederich, Founder of Synanon

Your life is an empty book with 1,000 blank pages. Only you determine how it will be written. Take charge of your future today. Be creative, professional, and enthusiastic—and someday you will enjoy reading your autobiography.

Gain Exposure, Gain Experience

Internships, co-ops, practicums, and part-time jobs related to your field of study are excellent and should be considered by every student. Often, these opportunities may not offer glamorous positions with the responsibility you desire, but participating in the environment can still be quite valuable. The experiences and contacts you gain will be helpful, and it certainly won't hurt your resume. This "preview" may also help clarify whether you really want to enter that field in the first place.

If you want an internship that you can truly gain value from, you have to approach the search similar to that of a job. It often takes research, networking, resume writing, etc. As you will find, this entire exercise will be great practice for the same skills you will need after graduation.

Target the company, industry, or position that would best meet your goals. What company would be most beneficial to you, and look the most impressive on your resume? What specific position within that company intrigues you the most? Contact that company to see what internships it may offer. Utilize the resources provided at the end of this chapter, in addition to those at your university career center or academic advising office.

Internships enable you to get a feel for *what it's really like vs. what is portrayed on TV* for many occupations. For instance, lawyers rarely argue a different murder trial every Tuesday, and doctors rarely perform emergency bypass surgery on a celebrity every Thursday. As an ambitious political science major in undergraduate school, I was honored to land an internship with United States Congressman James Talent. The excitement, notoriety, and influence of that position sparked dreams of going into politics myself someday. But after a semester of watching the laborious and frustrating day-in, day-out demands of an elected government official, I decided that was something I definitely DID NOT want to do.

When participating in an internship, work hard, make an impression, and really try to learn from people. Don't just be an innocent bystander. Pick people's brains. Ask employees about why they chose that career, and if they are happy they did. Are they confident about the growth of that field in the future? What things might they have done differently? Most professionals are more than willing to share their opinions and experiences with interns.

Make sure you get a letter of thanks or recommendation from the highest officer you worked with in the company. Keep it for your future interview portfolio. It is important to illustrate that you didn't just show up every day to make copies, but you made some sort of contribution that was appreciated by key members of the organization. Make sure you are able to describe what responsibilities you had and what you accomplished. If that list seems unimpressive, further list projects that the department completed during your stint that you were able to learn from—even if you had a very limited role.

Make sure you let that company know you appreciated the experience and the opportunity. Feel free to keep in touch with those contacts periodically. This is when your professional networking begins. Certainly, if there is a future opportunity and a mutual fit, a good internship could translate into a full-time position, as well. Even if the company doesn't have a position available for you, your contacts might know a colleague who does.

An increasing number of college graduates now work at least part-time in an unrelated environment while earning their degree. This leaves even less time to devote to hands-on experience options. However, if at all possible, try to invest in your future with one of these opportunities. There are also other ways to get hands-on experience in the field you are considering, such as volunteering or even job-shadowing a position for a day.

The point is, it's imperative to explore and gain exposure to certain jobs beforehand. It helps you truly understand the day-to-day tasks you need to become accustomed to every day for years to come. If you find that you are indeed turned off by what you experience, discuss other career options with an advisor, or even another area of study. Investing a few extra credit hours, or even a few extra semesters, earning a different degree might be worth it to you. There's no sense entering a field you dislike.

Recommended Books

Internships 2005 (Peterson's Internships)
Peterson's, 2004

The Internship Bible
Princeton Review, 2004

Scoring a Great Internship (Students Helping Students)
Ellen Rubinstein – Natavi Guides, 2002

Recommended Websites

http://wetfeet.internshipprograms.com
www.Vault.com
www.internships.com
www.rsinternships.com
www.internjobs.com
www.internship4america.com
www.princetonreview.com/cte/search

Study Something You Like

For many of you reading this, it could be too late to change your major or area of emphasis. I have spoken at many university functions, including freshman orientation, and have always made a plea for young students to pursue their interests. You will be doing yourself a favor for the rest of your life.

College students frequently take three routes when deciding upon a major:

1. They study something they are interested in, and try to figure out what to do with that degree later.

2. They select a major they think has practical value of getting them a job, whether they like it or not.

3. They are undecided or keep switching majors, seeking a fit between 1 and 2.

I was so inspired by my freshman political science class, I decided to switch majors after my first semester. I wanted to learn more about politics and government. I performed better in those courses the rest of the way, even though they were more difficult. I also combined all of my electives within the same major, and earned a second B.A. degree in communications. Those classes were fascinating to me, as well. So, what classes do you enjoy? In what subjects do you excel?

If you study something you like, you are more likely to attend class, pay more attention in class, get better grades, and have a greater chance of graduating. You will then have a more enjoyable four years of college. This will also lead you into a career of doing something you enjoy for the next 40 years. In the next chapter, we will examine how there is much more hope than you might think regarding building a successful and fulfilling career around your true interests.

If you study something you don't like, you might be wasting four years of gaining knowledge and a degree in a field you will soon leave because you can't stand what you do. But alas, if this is the case, there is still more hope than you may think to turn your "wasted" degree into a success, so do not despair.

It is amazing to me how many people have gone so far astray in their careers from the degrees they originally earned. The stories are countless, and you may know of some yourself. I have several close friends from college who went entirely different directions, and successfully. They include:

- *A criminal justice major who is a salesperson for an information technology company.*
- *A psychology major who negotiates pricing for a major aviation company.*
- *A communications major who went into auto sales, then auto dealership management.*
- *An industrial technology major who is a loan officer at a mortgage company.*
- *A political science major who owns a business performance improvement company (that's me!)*

As you can see, there is always hope, even if you find out later your "calling" is different from the original curriculum you studied. However, the earlier you can identify what your "calling" or area of interest might be, the greater head start you will have.

Do Something You Like

This is the first major lesson and piece of advice in this book, because it is that important to your future success and happiness. Do something you like. One of the biggest shames in America today is how many people are miserable where they work. It is probably the single greatest contributor to unhappiness in this country on a daily basis.

"I hate my job."

"I hate my boss."

"I hate my clients."

"I'm tired, frustrated, and I had a miserable day."

Of course, one lesson the previous section illustrates is that it's never too late to switch to a field you didn't study in college. If you are presented with another opportunity you find exciting, consider it! The good thing is, you are still young. You may feel that switching fields wastes that college degree and extensive experience you gained between the ages of 23 and 25. But in the big picture, you could still become an expert in something else you enjoy and devote the next 40 years of your life to it.

> *"If you find a job you love,*
> *you will never work a day in your life."*
> - Confucius

I have interviewed countless candidates for various positions over the past 10 years. Depending on the position, you'd be surprised how little I actually considered what specific degree a candidate had earned. There are plenty of attributes that are proven simply from earning a college degree, no matter what the major. First, it shows employers that you successfully completed four years of advanced study. Many fail, so congratulations! It also shows that you learned, wrote papers, completed projects, beat deadlines, fulfilled responsibilities, and hopefully took part in many other activities that helped you grow personally.

Employers are looking for professional, talented, responsible candidates who can perform the duties of a specific job. Sometimes there are specific degree requirements for positions, but often there are not. This allows you to consider opportunities in a much wider scope than you may have previously believed possible.

The harsh reality is that the average American spends more than twice as many waking hours at work than with family and friends. Think about that.

If the average person sleeps eight hours per night, and works eight hours per day, that means two-thirds of one's life consists of sleeping and working. That leaves the final one-third of one's life to consist of everything else. Of course, the final one-third also includes such things as traffic (to and from work), lunch (while at work), and working extra hours (yes, also done at work). So how many working hours does just the basic eight hours per day actually equal?

40 hours per week x 52 weeks = 2,080 hours!

2,080 hours per year x 40 years = 163,200 hours!

Sound depressing? Well, it will be if you devote your life to something you don't like. In fact, you will be absolutely miserable. Hence, the title of this section.

I had so many friends that simply did not like their job after college. I have seen way too many other people of all ages over the last 10 years who hated their job. It affected their entire life—horribly. Watching them affected me so much that it contributed to my inspiration for writing this book in the first place. Trust me, it is not worth it.

Perhaps these people felt trapped. Their education and experience may have led them down a path to a particular position or industry. Perhaps they didn't appropriately consider studying or pursuing something they enjoyed in the first place. Why did they take that first job originally, and why did they stay there? You are never stuck—you will always have options.

I also knew too many people who spent the majority of their 20's floundering around on a lost career path. When I would run into them periodically at a social function, it would always be something different:

"No, I'm not doing that anymore—it was stupid. Now I'm studying for my Series-7, because my cousin can get me a job as a broker and he's raking it in."

When I would see them six months later, they would say:

"No...Actually, I'm going to back to school now to work on my psychology degree."

This would continue for five years. Don't waste five years of your life! Start building your career now and be five years ahead of all these people. There are a lot of them out there.

Consider not only what career you might enjoy, but also what environment. What about a job that is outdoors, or involves animals, or sports and entertainment? There are plenty of resources available for careers in each of these specific areas. Would you enjoy a position that involves travel? Often, young professionals relish the opportunity to travel and "see the world" while they have the chance. A few years later, many are inclined to settle down, either for family reasons, a desire for a more stable working environment, or because they simply get tired of the rigors of travel. Ideally, that field experience can lead them into a promotion at the corporate office.

I know of many people who opted against pursuing certain fields they might have enjoyed because they are not considered to be lucrative. Such careers include teaching, journalism, social services, or athletic coaching. However, there are countless examples of financially successful people in each of those fields—well beyond your imagination. And if that may seem like a long shot to achieve, you can earn an above-average salary for your profession within the first five years, if you do the right things. You need to be dedicated, be good at what you do, and follow the steps of career promotion illustrated in the later chapters of this book.

Teachers, for instance, can gain expertise within their teaching level (elementary, secondary, university). By becoming truly good at what they do, there is the opportunity to win awards, earn raises, and secure higher paying positions in better schools. Teachers can submit articles to trade journals, write a book, or even produce their own textbook. Teachers can also use summers wisely for extra earnings potential, which is a terrific advantage in that profession.

There is always greater income potential in teaching at the collegiate level. According to the National Center for Education Statistics, the average four-year university professor earns over $80,000 annually. Not a bad living, especially considering additional avenues available to professors to increase their income throughout the year. There is always the opportunity for a teacher in elementary education to teach others about the subject at the collegiate level, either part-time or full-time.

For journalists, the Internet has provided a medium for articles and columns to be read around the world, not just in one locale. There are tremendous freelance opportunities available, and a myriad of publications and websites where articles can be published or reprinted for cash. This can all be in addition to one's "day job."

One final example is athletic coaching. Performance, or record, is particularly emphasized for advancement in this position. If coaches are good at serving as assistants, they can earn a head coaching position. If head coaches excel in high school or small college, they can continue to work their way up. If they can become one of 300+ Men's Division I college football or basketball coaches, the rewards can be quite lucrative. The average salary well exceeds $200,000, and that balloons to an average of $1.1 million for a Top 20 collegiate program, according to a 2002 USA Today special report. Each college also has numerous assistants who don't make near the head coach's salary, but still make a healthy living.

Even if a coach never makes it to that level, there are camps, books, instructional videos, off-season coaching opportunities, and other profitable endeavors, not to mention combining coaching duties with teaching courses at the same school.

Always consider additional opportunities for income within your profession. Most professions have such opportunities, but few take advantage of them because of time, effort, or simply being unaware of what alternatives are available. The main point here is that you should have hope and encouragement, no matter what field you choose. Believe that you can lead a rewarding, successful, and prosperous career—because you can. It's all up to you.

Now, stop and picture yourself being able to witness people at your funeral. That's right. Close your eyes and imagine that scene.

> **?** *What do you want people to say about you?*
>
> **?** *How would you want your eulogy to read?*
>
> **?** *What will be written on your gravestone?*
>
> **?** *Will you be proud of your livelihood?*
>
> **?** *Will you be proud of your accomplishments?*

What *do* you want to be remembered for? That you dedicated your life to impacting the lives of other people, or that you dedicated your life to help ACME Manufacturing sell millions of widgets?

This may be an admittedly unfair comparison, as many of us *(including me)* dedicate ourselves to companies who provide and sell a product or service. We may seek defining characteristics outside of our career, such as family, voluntarism, writing, athletics, or hobbies. However, do you realize the vast majority of lifetime accomplishments are achieved after college graduation? This means 50 years from now no one will remember or care about what you have done so far. Only this point forward will define your person, your life, and what people remember about you. Therefore, truly consider pursuing careers that impact what you believe in, what you have conviction in, or what you possess a true love in. You just may find it to be *very* rewarding.

While this may seem to be a morbid exercise to impact your career choices, choices, it may provide a different perspective those graduating college don't often ponder. Often, college graduates are concerned with simply getting a job. This is your first big decision on your road to happiness. Choose wisely.

So, what do you like? What are you interested in? What field might be a good match for your skill set? Career assessments, such as the Myers-Briggs Type Indicator®, SIGI PLUS®, the Strong Interest Inventory®, and other tools and exercises can provide valuable assistance for you in this area. These items should be available at your career center or university library. It's never too early to try to figure out what you want to do with your life. More information on this is provided at:

www.life-after-college.com/assessments

From a career standpoint, you may only pursue one field to which you will dedicate your entire life. Decide on a road, keep driving, and never stop. If you are good at what you do, and have a focused career plan, you can be successful and make a good living doing almost anything. Thus, do something you like and go for it.

Recommended Books

What Color Is Your Parachute? 2005:
A Practical Manual for Job-Hunters and Career-Changers
Richard Nelson Bolles – Ten Speed Press, 2004

What Should I Do With My Life: The True Story of
People Who Answered the Ultimate Question
Po Bronson – Random House, 2003

Do What You Are: Discover the Perfect Career for You
Through the Secrets of Personality Type
Paul Tieger and Barbara Barron-Tieger
Little, Brown & Company, 2001

How Important Is Money To You?

Everyone has their own values and beliefs about money. In general, our society places a high priority on money. Money, money, money. Sometimes it seems it's all about the money. But there are many things to consider when searching for that perfect career, and money is only one factor. Those who hold out for merely the highest initial job offer are often misguided. Be careful with your decision here.

The relationship between money and happiness is one of the most elusive and intriguing issues in our society today. Often people spend a lifetime battling with themselves for their own interpretation of the answer.

Do you consider yourself happy right now? You may.

How much money do you make? Any?

I knew plenty of people who had a blast in college, including me, and we made $9.00 per hour waiting tables working 20 hours per week. We drove humble cars (*at best*), and were always on the lookout for Taco Bell® coupons, so we could eat lunch for less than $3.00. So, why were we so happy?

The experiences you have, the relationships you share with friends and loved ones, and the time you devote to things you enjoy define your happiness. Perhaps even emotions such as a sense of accomplishment, and doing things that are rewarding play a role as well. Another source of my happiness in college came from achieving good grades and fulfilling responsibilities in campus organizations. In my career, contributing to the success of companies and impacting people's lives are things that provide me a rewarding sense of accomplishment, and that brings me happiness.

Unfortunately, we live in a society where we are just never satisfied. You may consider it "*keeping up with the Jones's.*" Or, you may consider it trying to satisfy our ongoing personal craving for material wants and needs. You might love your 25-inch TV for a couple of years, but then you want to upgrade to the 32-inch TV, because that will make you happy. You love that new TV even more, until you start to fall in love with the 50-inch FLAT SCREEN TV every time you walk into the electronics store. You've got to have that FLAT SCREEN TV! People are the same with houses, cars, boats, computers, shoes—and yes—salaries!

> $ *When you make $30,000, you will want to make $35,000.*
>
> $ *When you make $35,000, you will want to make $40,000.*
>
> $ *When you make $40,000, you will want to make $50,000.*
>
> $ *When you make $50,000, you will want to make $70,000.*
>
> $ *When you make $70,000, you will want to make $100,000.*
>
> $ *When you make $100,000, you will want to make $200,000.*

This process will continue until your goal is to equal the net worth of Bill Gates, which you will never hit. You will then consider yourself a failure and live a life of depression.

Don't get caught up in the bragging and competition with your friends of "*So, how much money do you make?*" My advice is to keep a firm grasp on the big picture of your career and what you value. You may find it tough, but sacrificing a "few thousand bucks" per year for a position that offers you personal development and future opportunity is well worth it. Many good entry-level positions provide outstanding experience, allowing you to eventually leapfrog others who make more money now in jobs that are either dead-end, or jobs they are miserable doing but are afraid to admit.

Getting caught up in such competition can be damaging to your priorities and your perspective, throwing out of balance the relationship between money and happiness. Others may believe the competition to "keep up" encourages a greater drive to succeed and helps squelch complacency. There might be merit to both lines of thought. Just remember the word "balance."

Often I will hear a college student say "*I want to make a lot of money.*" I enjoy engaging them in this conversation. I will first ask "*Why?*" This trick question often provokes thoughtless answers, or simply renders them speechless. Next I might ask "*How much is a lot of money?*" I have heard answers ranging from $25,000 to $1,000,000 per year. Consider that for a moment.

The answer "*a lot of money*" is relative.

If they answer, say, $100,000 per year, I will then ask:

> *"Will that amount of money make you happy?"*
> *"Yeah."*
> *"What if you made $150,000 per year? Would that make you even more happy?"*
> *"Yeah!"*
> *"But, if you were only making $90,000 per year, you wouldn't be happy?"*
> *"Ummm…"*

Washington Post columnist Michelle Singletary examined a 2002 study conducted by Jean Chatzky, with the help of Money magazine and RoperASW. More than 1,500 people were surveyed investigating the relationship between salary and happiness.

Singletary surmised that *"74 percent of those earning less than $25,000 a year said overall they were somewhat or very happy with their lives. There is a 10 percentage point jump in the happiness factor between people earning $25,000 and $50,000. But after $50,000, the overall happiness of respondents did not increase that much. The survey showed that 84 percent of people earning $50,000 or more were happy with their friendships, standard of living, marriage, children and appearance. Eighty-six percent of people earning $100,000 reported they were satisfied with their lives. Chatzky concluded that income, to the extent that it makes you comfortable, does contribute to your happiness. But once you've achieved basic comforts, your happiness has to come from another source."*

"Of course, money plays a role in the happiness equation," concluded Jean Chatzky. *"To try to deny that link would be disingenuous, not to mention unbelievable. But it's not as strong a link - as big a contributing factor - in your happiness as you might think."*

This parallels Abraham Maslow's "hierarchy of needs" theory. As many business and psychology majors study, Maslow determined that once people achieve a basic state of security with relation to income, they seek other sources for life happiness and fulfillment. Related findings from a study at the University of California-Berkeley were released in the June 2003 issue of *Personality and Social Psychology Bulletin*.

"In a capitalistic society, people generally believe that - all other things being equal - being rich is better," said Haas School of Business Professor Jennifer Chatman. *"But that is not what we found."*

By no means do I want to discourage people from wanting to "make a lot of money." I encourage everyone to aim high and set goals in their lives, especially financial goals. To a certain extent, it is that drive that also pushes us to perform harder or better in what we do. Just be sure to keep the pursuit of money in appropriate balance with the rest of your life. Do not make money the primary source of your self-worth and happiness, or you will never be satisfied.

As examined, young people frequently struggle with the question "Should I do something I like or do something that I can make more money in?" Ideally, the answer can be both. It can certainly be both more often than you may think. When you are happy doing what you do, it is amazing what good things will happen. You are willing to work harder because you enjoy what you are doing. You stay involved with your field because you enjoy what you are learning. You do a better job because you take pride in your work. These are the very attributes that breed success in a career, and lead to making more money, anyway, correct?

Recommended Books

You Don't Have to Be Rich: Comfort, Happiness, and Financial Security on Your Own Terms
Jean Chatzky – Portfolio, 2003

The 100 Simple Secrets of Happy People
David Niven – Harper San Francisco, 2003

How to Be Happy at Work:
A Practical Guide to Career Satisfaction
Arlene S. Hirsch – JIST Publishing, 2003

Chapter Two:

The Job Search

Be Selective When Choosing A Job

In researching for this book, I was amazed that 90% of books on this general topic describe how to write resumes, interview, and "get a job." At the end of this chapter, I have listed numerous books and websites for you to use as a guide for such specific help. While this is certainly important, getting a job is not as important as getting the right job for you.

It's tough to be patient and selective when attempting to find your first job after graduation. The job market can be tough for recent graduates. You have pressure from yourself, pressure from parents, and pressure from friends. Everyone is asking *"So, do you have a job yet?"*

However, this is a BIG decision. Do you know you could be working for this company for the next 5, 10, 20 or 40 years? It could be much longer than the time you spent at one college—and think about how important that decision was. This decision is bigger! Remember, you will spend more of your waking hours inside the four walls of that company than you will anywhere else. Be sure whatever position you choose is right for you.

Things To Consider With Job Selection Include:

☞ **Salary** *(Can you negotiate? Are there bonuses?)*

☞ **Advancement Opportunity** *(What is the natural jump from that position, and what is the normal time frame?)*

☞ **Personal Development** *(Will they develop you? Will this experience help launch you into better positions?)*

☞ **Job Responsibilities** *(Are you clear about what type of work you will be doing? What is a typical day?)*

☞ **401k/Retirement Plans** *(Do they match investment?)*

☞ **Health Benefits** *(HMO? PPO? Dental? Do you need special coverage for prescriptions, pre-existing conditions, or other family members?)*

☞ **Hours/Schedule** *(Vacation Policy? Typical overtime?)*

☞ **Geographic** *(Relocation? Travel? Traffic? Commute?)*

What do you really know about the company that has a job opening you are considering? What is the outlook for its industry? Financially, how healthy is the company? Is it growing? What are its challenges? How is its employee satisfaction? Does it have a high turnover rate? If so, why? Would you be replacing someone, or is the company expanding? If they are replacing someone, why did the last person leave? Were they overwhelmed, sick of the job, or promoted?

It is very important to look closely at the benefits package a company offers, including 401k, profit sharing, stock purchase plans, and medical/dental insurance. Have someone you trust advise you, or refer to the references at the end of this chapter for assistance. The company HR manager should be able to explain any questions you may have, as well.

According to *dictionary.com*, a 401k is:

"A retirement investment plan that allows an employee to put a percentage of earned wages into a tax-deferred investment account selected by the employer."

Some employers will "match" the percentage of salary you decide to invest each period. For instance, if you decide to save 3% from every check to invest, the company would also invest 3% for you, giving you a 6% total investment. Typically, there are caps on how much each company will match, which is an important percentage to know. It is highly recommended to at least invest up to the amount your company will match.

It takes self-discipline to participate in your 401k. However, let's say that you will invest 3%, and your company will match 3%, while your annual salary is $35,000. According to <u>thebeehive.org</u>, which uses a typical "401k calculator," you would accumulate $587,540 over the next 40 years. Of course, that figure should be quite conservative, considering future salary (and subsequent investment) increases throughout your career.

As I learned later, vacation time is particularly important to me because of my lifestyle and what I value. At the time, I didn't even know what the vacation policy was until a week after I took my first job! By the time I jumped to my second company, I realized that vacation was important enough to me that I would negotiate for additional days off, and I got them. As a manager, I found that negotiating vacation with a candidate was easy, because it doesn't put a dent in my budget at all. *(Although, fellow employees and HR managers don't appreciate such "unfair" inconsistencies!)*

Further, you should ask about smaller factors, such as the company dress policy and company perks. Often perks are a terrific way for companies to offer low-cost or no-cost products or privileges to keep employees happy. *(Tip: If you are interviewing at Anheuser-Busch or Coors, don't ask them if you can get free beer.)* Is the company dress code business casual, or will you need to purchase a new formal wardrobe? If it is casual or business casual, ask for written guidelines upon accepting the position, so you don't look too stupid your first day.

The most important questions you need to ask yourself before accepting a position are:

? *"Will I enjoy doing this?"*

? *"Is this a right first step for my career?"*

? *"Where will this position take me?"*

Do not take a job just to take a job. What is another two months of searching if it saves you years of being stuck in the wrong position? Don't accept a position with the attitude, "Well, I can always quit after a week if I don't like it." This is not Al's Pizzeria. This is the real world, and that philosophy will burn professional bridges and earn you a poor reputation quickly.

Recommended Books

Talking Money : Everything You Need to Know About Your Finances and Your Future
Jean Chatzky – Warner Business Books, 2002

401(k)s for Dummies
Ted Benna, Brenda Watson Newmann – Wiley, 2002

Maximizing Your Health Insurance Benefits
Richard Epstein – Praeger Publishers, 1997

Recommended Websites

www.youngmoney.com
www.401khelpcenter.com
www.insweb.com/learningcenter

Target Marketing

Target marketing is a concept I feel is the most important, effective, and often overlooked method of finding a job. It has been estimated that only 10% of the job openings in a metropolitan area are listed in the employment section of the newspaper. Yet, many job-seekers methodically scroll through those Sunday paper listings, and tediously comb the Internet, trying to rationalize why some off-the-wall position is for them.

☺ 3rd shift maintenance supervisor at the zoo *("I like pets")*
☺ Industrial equipment sales *("I know what a forklift is")*
☺ Dental office manager *("I have teeth")*

Instead, you decide what companies you want to work for, then seek and destroy. Again, get picky! Where do you want to work? What industry, what company, and what position?

Don't make the assumption that there are only three companies in your area that do what you want to do. In other words, chemistry majors shouldn't just target the three chemical companies in their city. There are thousands of companies who need that background in some part of their organization. They may range from food companies, to medical, to manufacturing. The same goes for technical positions, marketing, management, etc. These can be applied most anywhere.

There should be at least 10 companies you should target within the city you want to work. Research them on the Internet and learn everything you can about those companies. You may find that will "weed out" some companies and narrow down the list of those you feel will be right for you. It will also give you valuable knowledge of those companies that may help you get a position. Most of these companies have their employment opportunities posted on their website already. Surprise—these same opportunities are probably not also posted in the Sunday paper.

How do you identify the most ideal opportunities for your future? What opportunities will provide job security and increasing demand in the future? Be strategic, and research:

➯ *What products and services are growing?*
➯ *What industries are growing?*
➯ *What companies are growing?*
➯ *What positions are growing?*

Material to answer these questions should be available in your university career center, or you can utilize the resources provided at the end of this chapter. Regarding the fields you are interested in, which ones are growing or dying in the future? Hopefully, this is something you considered when you originally decided upon a major.

A December 2003 article from *Money* magazine identifies several U.S. positions that will be slowly vanishing by 2015, according to a study by Forrester Research. Such jobs include financial underwriters, computer programmers, software engineers, paralegals, and travel agents.

Every year, *Fortune* magazine produces its list of the *"100 Best Companies to Work For"* in America. Do any of them have locations in your area? Are any of them in your field? Research what companies you are interested in to see if they ever made the list in previous years. Fortune also has lists for the *"100 Fastest-Growing Companies,"* the *"Small Business 100,"* and the *"50 Best Companies for Minorities."*

If you are willing to relocate, consider what metropolitan markets are growing, especially for your industry. A study in the March 2004 issue of *Business 2.0* magazine listed America's 20 hottest job markets. The list was led by Raleigh-Durham, which has a projected job growth of 14% by 2008, including a healthy percentage of high-wage jobs.

As prudent as such research may be, do take the forecasts with a grain of salt. Don't become too discouraged if your field of interest is projected to shrink. Is the reason for shrinking technology-based, where the demand for such products and services will be eliminated in the future? Or, are the trends simply cyclical?

Remember, people who predict the future are not always right. If they were, we would all be driving small, economical Japanese cars according to experts of the 1970's and 1980's. Instead, we crave spacious, expensive, gas-guzzling SUV's! If a field is supposed to shrink from 610,000 jobs to 550,000 jobs in the next 10 years, that isn't necessarily cause to run to your academic advisor and switch majors, as 550,000 jobs are still a lot. And, with the retirement of baby-boomers in the workforce, many positions in almost every field will be needing replacements. So, be wise, but do not despair.

While you're at it, you may want to research specific jobs that have particularly good salaries, good hours, or good fringe benefits. For instance, there are many easier paths to success and happiness than you might believe. There are millions of Americans who work long, hard hours every day for 40 years, and for humble salaries. Yet, there are non-traditional occupations that often provide better hours, better pay, and just may match your skill set. Wouldn't you rather be considered "overpaid" than "underpaid"?

In the November 6, 2003, *CBS MarketWatch* article "Ten Most Overpaid Jobs in the U.S.," writer Chris Plummer listed major airline pilots, wedding photographers, and orthodontists, just to name a few. *Money Magazine* produced a two-part series "Who Gets Paid Six Figures" in January 2004, in which writer Jeanne Sahadi listed additional lucrative surprises. They include retail home fashion consultants, home-based broadcast captioners, and video game artists. Just for fun, visit www.6figurejobs.com to see what types of positions in what industries are actually being sought out for top dollar, and what the desired experience and qualifications are.

Have you ever run into someone with such a unique career and wondered:

"So, how in the world does someone get to do that for a living?"

Let's consider the wedding photographer, for example. I intentionally picked a career for this exercise I knew nothing about—(As proof, I have never been married, nor have I ever owned a camera). After researching for just two hours using the Internet, online access to my public library, and a phone call to a recent photographer of a friend's wedding, I now know:

- *The average salary of wedding photographers, part-time and full-time.*
- *The difference between independent photographers, photography studios, and photography agencies.*
- *The options of 6-month certification training programs and 4-year art and design school degree programs.*
- *A typical wedding photographer day/week.*
- *The timeline/process of a typical client.*
- *How wedding photographers develop a client base, and how they charge clients.*
- *The future of wedding photography services, such as online animated photo albums and custom wedding websites.*
- *The U.S. Department of Labor projects that the demand for photographers is to rise 17% by the year 2010.*

You could simply start "on the side" with such opportunities first to determine if you enjoy it, if you are good at it, and if there is enough profitable opportunity to do it full-time. Or, you can just keep it as a hobby to earn extra income in addition to your "real job."

The bottom line is, there are many alternatives to consider if you want to target an "off-the-beaten path" career with such lifestyle or financial advantages. You are still young enough to be anything you want if you put your mind to it.

Recommended Books

Wedding Photography 101: The Complete Guide to Starting and Growing a Wedding Photography Business
Scott Harris – 1st Books Library, 2004

The Wedding Photographers' Book of Contracts, Policies, Procedures
Steve Herzog – Incite Publications, 1995

Professional Marketing & Selling Techniques for Wedding Photographers
Jeff Hawkins, Kathleen Hawkins – Amherst Media, 2001

Recommended Website

http://www.photography-schools-colleges.com/

Recommended Magazines

Popular Photography   *Photo Techniques*
American Photo   *Shutterbug*

What Type Of Company Fits You?

So, what size company should you target? What would be a good fit for you? I have been fortunate within my first 10 years to be employed by a large, medium, and small company, and have also dealt plenty with the public sector along the way. I believe working for a large corporation in the beginning of my career helped later on, because it gave me additional credibility. Almost everyone had heard of the big company I worked for, and it had a good reputation in the community and the business world. There were also much greater opportunities for promoting from within, as opposed to a smaller company where there may not be as much room to grow.

A big company allows you to work with many contacts in many different fields, who are either internal employees in other departments or external clients and vendors. Big companies will also typically provide quality in-house training programs and expose you to the latest in cutting-edge technology and industry trends.

Budgets can be in direct proportion to the size of a company. For instance, while a $3,000 travel expense for a trade show might be a huge pill to swallow for a small company, it may be a drop in the bucket for a large one. There may also be advantages in benefits and other perks offered by larger companies, such as stock options, health plans, matching 401k contributions, and negotiated discounts within the community.

Lastly, there can be great compensation packages awaiting if you are able to advance to the highest positions within a large corporation. At companies with sales of at least $35 billion in the United States and Europe, CEOs earn an average salary and bonus of $2.4 million, according to a study conducted by the Hay Group in a February 2004 *Business Week* article. Keep in mind, though, this won't happen overnight. The youngest *Forbes 2000* CEO is 38-year old Richard J. Dugas, Jr., head of Pulte Homes, and the average CEO age is 56.

Ironically, one reason why I chose my first employer was that it was a big corporation, and I wanted job security. You know, small businesses go out of business every day, right? This past year, that same big corporation went through its fourth major wave of layoffs within the past decade. It claimed the jobs of several very good friends and fellow workers I had there. So much for security.

There are several other downfalls to working with a large company. At times it may seem you're an inconsequential mouse in a maze of cubicles and offices and buildings. As important as you think you might be, the company would be absolutely unaffected by your departure. They would hire someone else, and the machine would keep churning as you become an immediate distant memory. This is a tough transition for a young go-getter who truly wants to make a difference in a company right away.

Would you rather be a big fish in a small pond?

I personally felt more at home in a smaller company. I reported directly to the president, had more responsibility, and had a direct impact on the company's success. To me, this was very rewarding. Salaries, bonuses, and days off were much more flexible and informal, which was fun. I remember six months after I began, the president of the company called me into his office and handed me a $1,500 check for *(basically)* no reason. This definitely wasn't part of my pay plan. It wasn't raise time, Christmas bonus time, or my birthday either. He just said he appreciated what I had brought to the company thus far, *"So, here you go."* Try getting that approved through HR as a manager in a large corporation!

There also might be less competition in smaller companies. Everyone is trying to get into the big ones, and many have inside connections because they are so big. There is a better chance for a team or "family" atmosphere within smaller companies. Everyone's role is important, and everyone shares in the problems, accomplishments, and celebrations together. Almost exactly 50% of all U.S. private sector jobs are within small businesses, which is defined as having less than 500 employees, according to the United States Small Business Association. The pros and cons of owning your own small business will be examined later in Chapter Eight: *Planning Your Ultimate Road to Success.*

Other major employers include non-profit organizations, public works, and the government, which is the largest employer in the United States. It is hard to generalize these jobs, since there are so many. There are typically set structures, policies, and salaries. The security of government positions is good, but that also contributes a slower advancement track. Government jobs do provide quality training, however they may not provide you with "cutting edge" trends or technologies. Administrative bureaucracy can be an environment slow to change.

Often, the rewards of achieving the highest levels of leadership within a government organization don't nearly compare to that of a private sector company. For instance, according to an April 30, 2004, report by *The Business Journal*, the CEO of the United States Postal

Service (USPS) earned "only" $172,000 in 2003. This is compared to $6.7 million and $19.1 million in combined salary and stock options for Hewlett-Packard and Verizon CEO's, respectively. Both of those private companies had similar revenues as the USPS, a smaller number of employees, and actually earned less of a profit in 2003.

The important thing is to understand and be aware of the differences in each of these organizations. Consider which of these environments and career tracks might be right for you, given the pros and cons of each. Include these considerations in the type of companies you will target for employment.

Resumes And Interviewing

You may notice that I postponed discussing resumes and interviewing until now. This is because you need to create a solid philosophy on what you want to do with your life, and what type of companies you want to work for first. Too many people start the process by "shotgunning" their resume all over the city, country, and the Internet. Then they see who fires back and they take it from there. This is an act of desperation, and often employers can sense that. The job is choosing you, instead of you choosing the job.

My advice on resumes begins by resuming the target marketing plan you have undertaken. Customize your cover letters and resumes for each company and position. Hiring managers don't want to see a generic resume that they know has been "shotgunned" all over the planet Earth. They want to know that you want to work at *that company*. So, cater to them, don't insult them.

I always kept at least three different versions of my resume handy. One version was tailored toward management, one toward marketing, and one toward training. Within each one of those fields, I would customize each resume for that particular position and company. Consider every line, and ask yourself *"Will this hiring manager care about that?"*

Don't just tell me what position you held, tell me what you accomplished or what might be relevant to me—the hiring manager. Don't just list what organizations you were a member of, tell me what responsibilities you had, what you accomplished, and what skills you gained. Try to be as tangible as possible in every line. Don't tell me customer service or sales improved when you worked somewhere. Tell me customer satisfaction or sales levels increased 11.4% during the 1st Quarter of 2004 and 16.9% the 2nd Quarter of 2004.

The impact GPA has on your job candidacy is debatable among hiring managers, and often depends on the industry. An outstanding GPA may be required for highly competitive positions or companies. It may also be necessary for entrance into better graduate programs, either now or down the road. Low or mediocre GPA's may be used by hiring managers to "weed out" or "narrow down" a list of candidates for positions with a high volume of resumes.

As a general rule of thumb, if you earned a 3.0 GPA or higher in college, include it. If you graduated with less than a 3.0, don't. More times than not, a well-rounded resume with a 3.0 GPA and extra-curricular activities or experience is more impressive than a 3.5 GPA with nothing else. Many hiring managers value the combination of "streetsmarts" plus "booksmarts," or social skills plus functional skills.

Always get a second opinion of your resume before you submit it. Obvious spelling or format issues have somehow slipped past about 20% of all applicant resumes I have ever reviewed, which is simply unacceptable.

"Is this how you are going to communicate with our clients?"

Once your resume is complete, and you have exact companies and positions you are shooting for, be creative and aggressive. Can't find out who the HR manager is? Visit them. Tell the receptionist you are there to drop something off for the HR manager, and wanted to know whom to address it to. They will tell you. Can't get through the receptionist for the follow-up call? Call after hours and get the company directory. Punch in the manager's name to get the direct extension. Then try back the next day to their direct line.

There are many tricks to getting through the "gatekeeper" to the actual decision-maker *(a classic battle salespeople fight everyday in the real world)*. But, if you are serious about wanting to work there, you have to go the extra mile. Effort alone won't get you the job, but it might make the difference in giving you the shot you need—an interview.

In the interview, tell the hiring manager that you have gone to school for four years, been involved in key organizations, and had an internship simply to prepare you to work for *that company*. Interview with a purpose. Be hungry, prepared, and confident. There are advantages to being young in the marketplace. Managers may hire someone with less experience, but who is enthusiastic and energetic. Capitalize on this.

After you have identified your target companies, you must push for any possible connection you might have at those companies. Even faint acquaintances can help while namedropping in an interview.

> *"I used to play softball with Steve Watkins. He works in your accounting department, right? Great guy."*

Believe it or not, this helps! Interviewers want to know you are a person, not another stranger who is applying for the same position. They are looking for people who can not only do the job, but who can fit in as part of the team. And if they think you have a relationship with someone in the company already, you have a head start on becoming a team member.

Therefore, do you know *anyone* in that company? Does anyone you know know *anyone* in that company? Are you *sure*? If you are really desperate to work there, you can "pull out all the stops" by asking someone in the company to lunch. Contact anyone in a related department, introduce yourself, and tell them that you are a recent college graduate who would love to learn more about the field from a seasoned professional. People will do anything for a free lunch, especially if the topic is to talk about themselves. Now you know someone in the company, and you can let the hiring manager know you *"just had lunch with Larry Smith last week."* You might just find out some interesting scoop on the company, as well.

You are now competing with thousands, even millions, of other job-seeking graduates who also have a degree. Remember, you have to be creative and aggressive if you want to succeed at getting the job you want, or anything else you want in your career.

Negotiating Salary

Most college graduates do not have much leverage to negotiate salary with their first job. The job market is demanding, and so many recent grads have similar credentials—a degree. Often, entry level jobs have a set starting salary—take it or leave it. Some have ranges commensurate with the qualifications of the candidate. Perhaps you have skills or credentials that set you apart. This may include outstanding academics at a top university, work-related experience, or extra-curricular achievements.

In conversation, try to learn how many applicants there are, and exactly what the employer is looking for. You have to be able to gauge your leverage. Are there many others just as qualified for the position? How much do they want or need you? How long have they been looking to fill the position? Are they having a hard time finding a qualified applicant, and they finally decide to make you the job offer? If so, you might have an opportunity here. Try to ask them for a salary range of the position first, before they ask you what your salary requirements are. Know what you are worth, but be sure it is based on fact.

Just be careful and realistic, especially with your first job offer. This skill of negotiation comes with experience. You will find that most of this book is about creating value throughout your career so that employers *want you*, and are willing to pay more for you. It's all about supply and demand.

Recommended Books

1000 Instant Resume Results
Diane Stafford, Moritza Day – SourceBooks, 2004

The Resume Handbook, Adams Media Corporation, 2003

e-Resumes: Everything You Need to Know About Using Electronic Resumes to Tap into Today's Hot Job Market
Susan Britton Whitcomb, Pat Kendall – McGraw-Hill, 2001

201 Best Questions to Ask on Your Interviews
John Kador – McGraw-Hill Trade, 2002

Best Answers to the 201 Most Frequently Asked Interview Questions
Matthew DeLuca – McGraw-Hill Trade, 1996

Recommended Website

www.life-after-college.com/resume-review

Be Resourceful: Utilize Every Resource

"Trying to get a job is a full-time job."

Fortunately for you, there is much more assistance and many more resources available today than there were just 10 years ago. Much of that can be attributed to the Internet, and the explosion of *"How To"* books over the past decade. Utilize these tools, as well as your college career center. Most career centers provide excellent resources on everything you need to get a job. However, you must be willing to use these resources and really "do your homework." Getting your first job is your responsibility, not career or placement services. You must take charge. It can be time consuming and take a tremendous amount of work. Be prepared.

Many schools survey graduates six months after graduation to determine their early success. Hopefully, you can review recent post-graduate reports from your university. What was the employment success rate? What were the most common methods of getting a job? How much are graduates making from your college, in your field? This information should be available. An example of an actual 2002 study from Virginia Tech University is shown on page 50.

There is a full section dedicated to networking in Chapter Seven: *Spectacular Career Development*. The importance of networking as it relates to landing your first position cannot be overstated. Simply examine the Virginia Tech study. These are powerful results! If you look closely, you will also find that networking and personal contacts have become even more important year after year.

There is no doubt that powerhouse employment sites such as *Monster.com*, *CareerBuilder.com*, and *HotJobs.com* are great resources because of the sheer volume of job listings. However, there is also an equally overwhelming volume of job-seekers that comb these sites daily—your competition. You have to find other avenues on the Internet to hunt as well. Local employment websites within the city you are targeting can help. Professional associations and industry-specific websites are also critical to investigate, such as *JournalismJobs.com* for journalists, or any of these websites for engineering job-seekers:

http://www.degreehunter.com/engineering_jobs.html
http://www.graduatingengineer.com/
http://www.aecworkforce.com/
http://www.engcen.com/
http://www.interec.net/

Make sure you search for industry-specific job websites in your field. A healthy list of books, websites, and other career guides are listed below. For additional resources and updated direct links, be sure to visit:

www.life-after-college.com/resources

Virginia Tech University
How grads found jobs:

Employed graduates were asked the method by which they found the job they accepted. For each method, you see the percentage of employed bachelor's degree recipients who found their jobs through that method.

	Class of 2002	Class of 2001	Class of 2000	Class of 1999
Personal contacts / networking	43.8%	40.0%	40.0%	35.2%
Had previous work experience with this employer	11.9%	8.2%	9.8%	11.7%
Job advertisement	7.5%	7.5%	8.0%	12.7%
Internet	9.2%	9.5%	9.4%	*
Career fair, job fair contact	**	**	**	11.4%
Career Services programs	16.5%	17.9%	22.2%	19.3%
Other	9.2%	16.3%	10.2%	9.4%
Don't know / refuse to answer	1.8%	0.5%	0.2%	0.4%

* new item as of 2000; not listed as a choice on the surveys for prior years
** deleted as a choice as of 2000 (would fall into "other" category)

Source: Virginia Tech University Career Center, www.career.vt.edu

Recommended Job Search Books

Job Hunting A to Z
Wet Feet Press, 2003

Career Guide to America's Top Industries
JIST Works, 2002

Best Entry-Level Jobs
The Princeton Review, April 2004

200 Best Jobs for College Graduates
Michael Farr – JIST Works, 2002

Enhanced Occupational Outlook Handbook
Michael Farr – JIST Works, 2004

Jobs Related Almanac
Barricade Books, 2002

The American Almanac for Jobs and Salaries
Avon, 2000

Guide to Internet Job Searching
Margaret Riley Dikel, Frances E. Roehm
McGraw-Hill/Contemporary Books, 2002

The Book of U.S. Government Jobs:
Where They Are, What's Available and How to Get One
Dennis V. Damp – Bookhaven Press, 2002

Recommended Job Search Websites

www.monster.com
www.hotjobs.com
www.jobweb.com
www.degreehunter.com
www.4jobs.com
www.jobbankusa.com
www.careersingovernment.com

www.careerbuilder.com
www.job-hunt.org
www.careerjournal.com
www.topusajobs.com
www.job-search-engine.com
www.usajobs.opm.gov

Recommended Career Fair Websites

www.careerfairs.com
www.cfg-inc.com
www.psijobfair.com

www.careerfair.com
www.jobexpo.com
www.nationalcareerfairs.com

Other Recommended Career-Related Websites

www.about.com/careers
www.quintcareers.com
www.onetcenter.org

www.collegegrad.com
www.bls.gov/oco

Chapter Three:

So, You Got a Job

The New Kid On The Block

Upon acceptance of your first job, prepare for your learning capacity and work ethic to be quickly accelerated. You must understand your specific job responsibilities, and train on those responsibilities. You must learn to function in your company's integrated business system. You will have to learn all company policies and procedures. You will also have to learn the names, titles, and responsibilities of all your co-workers, and of course, try to fit in with your co-workers as well. Basically, just try to focus on making it through your first week alive.

The second day on the job is when you should bring in pictures, desk décor, a small plant, and perhaps even your own customized mouse pad. You don't want to be too assuming upon arrival your first day, like you are moving in. Just bring yourself, and perhaps a nice carrying case. Besides, they may not have a place for you yet. You may have to wait until somebody quits, gets transferred, or kicks the bucket. If that's not the case, you may be assigned to the dusty office that has no phone or PC yet, and is filled with boxes and knickknacks because the storage closet is full.

If your company or manager is on the ball, they will have every-thing ready for you your first day. This includes business cards, your own phone extension, a configured PC, a new e-mail address, and a clean office or cubicle with your own nameplate on it. Regarding your fate of landing an office vs. a cubicle, well, good luck. Sometimes there is just no substitute for having the ability to close your door when you want. If you start with a cubicle, don't panic. It just gives you that much more to strive for in your career.

You will have at least an hour to set up your voice mail, arrange your e-mail preferences, and play with customizing the screen saver on your PC. You will also get about 20 minutes to raid the office supply cabinet. During this shopping spree, you can acquire pencils, pens, notepads, staplers, tape dispensers, and highlighters of every color. You name it, it's all yours. This will be the most exciting part of your first day.

On a serious note, it has already been impressed upon you how many hours you will spend in this working environment. Employees who work in a healthy, clean, pleasant environment enjoy their job more, and are in turn more productive. There have been great advances in the last several decades in the study of ergonomics. Be sure your desk, chair, keyboard, and PC are ideally situated to ensure that you are comfortable while you are working, and that everything is arranged for optimal performance. Here's another tip for your office or cubicle *(especially for guys)*: Buy some plug-in air fresheners, so your area doesn't smell like…well…*you* at the end of a long working day.

Of course, your first day will also include the ever-exciting tour of the company, and your manager should serve as the guide. On the tour, you will get acclimated to bathrooms, vending machines, and other essential landmarks. You will also endure a seemingly endless number of employee introductions, leaving you unable to remember anyone's name or job responsibility.

"…and this is Jill and Betty in accounting. See Jill for any reimbursements, and see Betty for any problems with your check. OK, and over here we have Dennis…"

Everyone will be checking out the new kid on the block. Smile, use great eye contact, and give them a firm handshake. Almost hourly, someone will ask you the stale question *"So, how do you like it so far?"*

Try not to use the same response every time.

You will be joined at lunch either by your new manager or designated co-workers. This is unless you receive the dreaded *"You're on your own for lunch; the cafeteria is on the first floor."* This means you will face the possibility of eating lunch by yourself, rekindling anxiety of a first day at a new school where you have no friends.

As part of your orientation, you will spend plenty of isolated time your first week completing many mundane but necessary chores, such as:

☞ *Completing HR, insurance, and benefit paperwork*
☞ *Watching company videos*
☞ *Reading client case studies*
☞ *Reviewing product brochures and promo material*
☞ *Reading computer system manuals*
☞ *Reviewing organizational charts*
☞ *Reading company policies*
☞ *Reviewing basic department reports*
☞ *Reading job procedure manuals*

And, of course, all of these items are in addition to being trained for your actual job.

Hopefully, you will receive an outlined training and orientation schedule in writing. Some companies have comprehensive orientation programs that last weeks or even months. Some may even have classifications such as "in-training," or structured "Manager-In-Training" programs. While valuable, lengthy training programs may seem tedious and boring at times. You may find yourself getting over-anxious, and asking *"When do I start doing something?"*

Other environments might not be so organized. Some companies or departments may be very short-handed and under heavy pressure to "throw you into the fire" your first day.

"The best way to learn is to just jump in and do it," your manager rationalizes as you are thrown to the wolves.

Unfortunately, this type of "training" may lead to frustration, mistakes, and early employee burnout. This also may be a sign that the company environment and culture is one of always scrambling, falling behind, and putting out fires. This is high stress potential. Management should create a situation that allows an individual to succeed, not doomed to fail.

Another common, informal method of training is teaming up with a more experienced employee in your position, sometimes for several days. It goes something like this:

Manager: *"I want you to meet Bob. Bob has been here 20 years. Bob is going to show you the ropes."*
Bob: *"Hi, I'm Bob."*

The plan is to sit with Bob, follow Bob around, and learn everything from Bob, until you are ready to fly on your own.

No matter the circumstances, the bottom line is there will be a lot to learn. And it is your responsibility to learn your job, not someone else's responsibility to teach you. Be prepared to devote extra hours to get up to speed right away. Be observant, and try to be a quick learner. Ask questions at every turn to make sure you are clear of what your job responsibilities are, and that you know how to do them.

Be confident in yourself and your abilities. EVERYONE had a first job and a first day at some point. So, don't be intimidated, and make a great first impression with everyone.

Recommended Books

Your First Thirty Days: Building a Professional Image in a New Job
Elwood N. Chapman, Robert B. Maddux – Crisp Publications, 1998

Find the Bathrooms First!:
Starting Your New Job on the Right Foot
Roy J. Blitzer, Jacquie Reynolds-Rush – Crisp Publications, 1999

How to Succeed in Your First Job: Tips for College Graduates
Elwood F. Holton III, Sharon S. Naquin – Publishers Group West, 2001

Be Patient, Be Humble

You may quickly realize that all of your achievements from college don't mean squat to anyone once you begin working. This is a...

"What have you done for me lately?" society, not...

"What did you do somewhere else before you came here?"

You start from scratch, with a clean slate, for better or for worse *(that's three clichés in one sentence, by the way)*. Awards, achievements, and even your GPA may have helped you get the job, but they won't help you do your job.

> *"It's not just about getting a job.*
> *It's what you do with the job after you get it."*

Your spectacular career development begins on day one. Now is when you start keeping score, and you are playing for keeps. Every resume you submit until you retire will detail the achievements you make from this point forward. That is how you are going to earn future raises and future promotions.

While you may be excited, energetic, and motivated to rush up the company ladder, you may begin your career with some harsh realities. Many call it *"paying your dues."*

Although you may think you have the knowledge to be CEO at 22 years of age, your company doesn't. Accept your job responsibilities, the good and the bad. One of the shocks of entering the real world to many college graduates is the lack of glamour and real responsibility involved in their job at times. You study for years about management theory, global economics, gear ratios, standard deviations, and the chemical imbalances of newborn rats, yet someone hired you to:

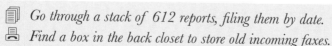

- Go through a stack of *612 reports*, filing them by date.
- Find a box in the back closet to store old incoming faxes.
- Drive across town to pick up a package for someone who actually is important.
- Cover the phones for the receptionists during their lunches and breaks.

You may find yourself saying:

> ☺ *"I went to college for this?"*
> ☺ *"I'm being underutilized."*
> ☺ *"I'm smart enough to do their job, and do it better!"*

You may be right! However, Rome wasn't built in a day. You simply have to keep pushing forward, and don't become discouraged. Often, these assignments are more necessary toward your learning and development than what you may believe. If you are asked to do filing, do the best filing you can do. If you are asked to answer customer phone calls, be the best customer representative you can possibly be. You have to make the most out of every position, even if it may not be your dream job just quite yet.

This is when people first take notice of your attitude, professionalism, and enthusiasm. Don't refuse or whine about duties or favors you may feel are beneath you. Everyone else in the company had to work their way up, too. Your day will come.

There was a terrific television commercial for FedEx featuring a young professional on his first day on the job at a new company. His boss walked in and said,

Manager: *"Hi, Tom, I know it's your first day, but we could really use your help."*

Employee: *"You got it,"* the young professional said as he confidently followed her down the hallway, spritzing his breath spray on the way.

Manager: *"Thanks, we're just in a bit of a jam,"* she said, as they came upon a large shipping area filled with boxes, and a computer monitor showing the fedex.com shipping screen. *"All this has to get out today."*

Employee: *"Yeah...uhhh... I don't do shipping."*

Manager: *"Oh, no, no, no....it's very easy. We use fedex.com. Anybody can do it."*

Employee: *"You don't understand,"* he chuckles arrogantly, then proudly replies: *"I have an M.B.A."*

Manager: *"Oh, you have an M.B.A. In that case I'll have to show you how to do it."*

Be prepared. Shipping may be in your future as well.

You Are Not Going To Believe What You See And Hear

Many newcomers are bright-eyed and positive, and ready to tackle the world...

"Wow! I finally got a job and I am going to tackle the world!"

"This company seems great, the manager who hired me seems great... seems like a great environment." Great.

It probably won't happen your first day, but perhaps by lunch hour of your third day, you will be taken aside by some "pros" who know it all. These "pros" are the ones who have been in the same position in the same company for 12 years, and blame everyone and everything else for why they are not CEO already. Their job is to give you the "scoop."

"This place sucks. Almost everybody is trying to get out. My resume is all over town."

"Our manager is a total jerk. He told me so many things in my interview, and none of them were true. Advancement opportunity my ass."

"Sales stink. I can't even believe they hired you—layoffs are right around the corner."

"Albertson is having an affair with his secretary. What a slimeball. He's got three kids. He tried to hit on me, too, but I told him to get lost."

"I can't believe they hired you into this position right out of college, when others had to work their way up. You're hated already, you know that, don't you?"

And when people quit or get fired, they don't say the most pleasant things on their way out.

"Get out while you can!"

"They're doing me a favor!"

"This place sucks anyway!"

Of course, some educated professionals in this environment have expanded their vocabulary even further to include other four-letter words that aren't even in the dictionary.

Quite a shock? You may have thought you left inappropriate environments in college, until you find out it gets worse!

Certainly, this does paint a poor picture. But this is not—*and should not be*—the norm in the professional working world today. Don't accept such examples as "the way it is," and do not get discouraged about the decision you made to work for your company. You can form your own opinion. Those phrases have been uttered by at least one bitter person in almost every company that has ever existed.

Witnessing gossip, unfounded rumors, backstabbing, foul language, people crying, and overall negativity is going to be a fact of life. Yet, look at it this way: The more negative people there are that surround you, the better you look if you stay positive and professional at all times. Eventually that will pay dividends.

Stay Positive

Working 40+ hours per week can be tough. You will experience many days where you are tired, not feeling well, overworked, and frustrated. You have to be a survivor in the working world. The best cure is to try to have fun at your job, and enjoy what you do every day. There is no better medicine than a good sense of humor at times, and no better release than an entertaining "take five" with a co-worker. Lighten things up! It is OK to laugh. That's what it's all about, remember? Do something you like.

If you are overworked for a period of time, keep faith that there is a light at the end of the tunnel. If you had a bad day, there is always tomorrow for a better one. Some people just don't see it that way. Americans must have something to complain about, right? Let others earn the reputation of being a whiner or complainer. It will drain energy and enthusiasm right out of you.

Negativity in the workplace is a common problem. It is human nature to think you should be paid more, work fewer hours, and have a better boss. Yet people need to be realistic, have a healthier attitude, and appreciate the positives about their job *(especially the fact that they have one)*. Stay focused on your job responsibilities and avoid getting pulled down by idle chatter.

Never get caught up in talking badly about your bosses behind their back. You will be sadly disappointed in the lack of loyalty your co-workers have when you believe your discussion is confidential. Besides, managers have a way of finding out what is *really* going on, and who is saying what.

Don't ever believe that outstanding job performance will make you exempt from firing because of attitude, misconduct, and personal conflicts with team members. There have been countless examples where top salespeople, top managers, or top athletes have been let go *(or traded)* because of these reasons. In 2003, the Tampa Bay Buccaneers told outspoken wide receiver Keyshawn Johnson to go home the rest of the season for undermining management. They paid him *not* to be around the team anymore. In the real world, employers will simply fire you. It is not worth it to them. Contrary to what you may think, you will ALWAYS be replaceable.

Staying positive also relates to days where it seems nothing is going right, you deal with problems that are out of your control, or even you yourself make a major mistake. Unfortunately, many graduates will enter high-pressure occupations or environments where these days are more common. Stress management is something you will have to practice and apply throughout your career.

Perhaps you will commit a major error that costs your company a lot of money. It could make you feel embarrassed, guilty, depressed, or incompetent for days. When this happens, you must remember that everyone makes mistakes. Take deep breaths, and keep the big picture of the problem in perspective. Stay confident in your abilities by remembering your positive attributes and past successes.

Never display negativity toward yourself in front of others, saying things such as *"I am so stupid."* However, it is OK to be honest: *"I made a mistake."* Consider what you can do to prevent that mistake from happening again. Be a stand-up person, not someone who tries to "pass the buck" to others. It's called taking responsibility for your actions, and people will respect that.

In examining all of my friends from college who were positive go-getters, I couldn't think of one who is still in an entry-level position, or one that has just bounced around from job to job, never getting anywhere. Yet, I guarantee all of them overcame failures, challenges, negativity, and criticism along the way.

"I'm not yelling at you, I'm giving you constructive criticism."

One of the keys to staying positive is learning how to accept criticism. It will come. It is impossible to go through your entire career without it. You simply have to distinguish between which are constructive criticisms that you can learn from and which are criticisms that stem from jealously or other questionable motives.

If criticism comes from a respectable source with sincere motives, have a healthy outlook of examining internally to see if there is anything you should approach differently. This is one way you can grow professionally. You don't have to be defensive or fire shots back. If you question the legitimacy or motives, turn the other cheek and hold strong to your confidence in the way you do things. Don't let them bring you down.

One thing I always considered when having to deal with others who didn't like the way I operated was presidential elections. Just think, George Bush and Bill Clinton both became President of the United States, yet more than 50 million people in this country voted *against* them. And you think you have critics? Try going to sleep at night in a country where 50 million people don't want you as their President. Somehow, I believe they were able to handle it just fine. You are always going to have critics. Just refocus yourself on your supporters and the people who believe in you. Most importantly, that should include you.

Recommended Books

101 Ways to Have a Great Day at Work
Stephanie Goddard Davidson – SourceBooks, 2004

The Power of Positive Thinking
Norman Vincent Peale – Ballantine Books, 1996

Managing Workplace Negativity
Gary S. Topchik – American Management Association, 2000

Be Professional, Not Immature

This is not Al's Pizzeria. You do not get mad at Al, take off your apron, roll it up in a ball, throw it at Al, and yell:

"This place sucks--I'm outta here!"

The perception of immaturity is a major barrier for young people to gain advancement within an organization. Frankly, there is often a good reason for that. Most young people are poor examples of professionalism and maturity. You must separate yourself from that. What organizations are always looking for are rising stars, future leaders, and management material. Will you elevate yourself from the pack of other young employees into one of these groups?

"Take the high road."

"Don't stoop to other people's level."

"Cooler heads must prevail."

"Can we discuss this like rational adults?"

Each of these clichés revolve around the struggle to maintain professionalism in a tense situation. There will be times throughout your career when your professionalism will be challenged. There are personal and professional differences that live within the walls of every company. It has been said that the true measure of a person is how they respond to adversity. People will ultimately respect rational and professional adult behavior. Upper management is looking for professionals to groom into management, not malcontents they have to continually discipline.

At the end of the day, everyone is still supposed to be on the same team. If you lose a promotion you think you should have gotten, congratulate that person. If it really was that close, you'll get the next one—if you stay professional. Nobody likes a sore loser. Be patient, because the cream will eventually rise to the top.

If your company is struggling or encounters a problem, how you handle yourself during the situation can define you as a professional. An immature professional considers it a catastrophe. A mature professional considers it a *"bump in the road."* An immature professional assigns blame and points fingers: *"That department screwed it up for us."* A mature professional views such things as a learning experience, and asks, *"How can we work better together in the future?"*

Emotionally reacting to a situation often stems from the pressure to do well, and in an odd way, illustrates you care. However, don't let your emotions get the best of you. Positive emotions can help channel energy and creativity in the workplace. Negative emotions can be a very dangerous barrier to team cohesiveness and success in the workplace.

Communication skills can prove to be an obvious distinction between a mature and an immature employee. When speaking in meetings and conference calls, it is wise to be courteous, articulate, and professional at all times. People will be constantly taking note of your tone and attitude when dealing with management, clients, or fellow employees. Tact and diplomacy must reign. Even when you reach a comfort level with your boss, referring to him as a "dude" or referring to her as a "gal" is just not appropriate.

Your professionalism is also constantly judged in your written communication, such as memos, reports, and especially e-mails. I have always had the habit, which is almost an obsession, of proofreading every e-mail I have ever sent in my life before clicking "Send." Continual e-mails with grammatical or punctuation errors give the impression that you are sloppy and unprofessional. Again, management will be thinking *"Is this how you communicate to our clients and customers?"*

College students often hear how important communication skills are to employers, and this is why. Hopefully, your education and background have prepared you to excel in this area. Being professional in your actions and your communications will allow you to advance much more quickly in your career.

Recommended Books

Victims, Villains and Heroes:
Managing Emotions in the Workplace
Don Phin, Loy Young – Aquarius House Press, 2002

True Professionalism: The Courage to Care About Your People,
Your Clients, and Your Career
David H. Maister – Free Press, 2000

Professionalism is for Everyone :
Five Keys to Being a True Professional
James R. Ball – Goals Institute, 2001

5 Steps to Professional Presence: How to Project Confidence,
Competence, and Credibility at Work
Susan Bixler, Lisa Scherrer Dugan
Adams Media Corporation, 2000

Recommended Seminars

"The Essentials of Communicating with Diplomacy
and Professionalism"
Skillpath Seminars, www.skillpath.com, 1-800-873-7545

"Self-Discipline and Emotional Control"
Fred Pryor Seminars, www.careertrack.com, 1-800-556-3009

"Business Writing and Grammar Skills"
National Seminars Group, www.natsem.com, 1-800-258-7246

Chapter Four:

Get Your Career Off to a Great Start

Be A Go-Getter And Impress Your Boss

One of the reasons some managers may hire a younger candidate or recent college graduate is that they believe this person has energy and motivation. They believe that what you may lack in experience, you can make up for with fresh ideas and enthusiasm. Don't disappoint them! This may have been the reason you got the job. Impress everyone, and go above and beyond the call of duty whenever possible. Exceed expectations with every project or responsibility. Set goals of trying to win company awards and earn promotions.

When considering strategies for career development and self-promotion, sometimes there is just no substitute for good old-fashioned hard work. You must be prepared to *earn* your way to the top. In this environment, people are watching and judging you 8+ hours per day. Managers monitor your work ethic closely, as well as your ability, your professionalism, and the quality of your performance. Especially in the beginning, nobody has more influence or control over your future than your direct manager.

Volunteer for special projects, committees, or extra-curricular clubs larger companies may sponsor. Contribute to solutions in the company that may or may not be your direct responsibility. Start developing ideas that might help your company advance in the future, be more efficient, or increase sales. Find a way to save your company money. Many companies actually have incentive plans available to employees who devise a way for the company to save money or increase profitability. Wow—not only can you impress the upper brass, but you can also earn bonus money while doing it.

By the way, don't feel that you can't save your company money. Trust me, there is plenty of opportunity here. Most companies *waste* tens of thousands, even millions of dollars on inefficiencies every year, whether they know it or not. They may include labor productivity issues, volume purchasing opportunities, freight/shipping inefficiencies, scrap/recycling programs, etc. You know, the stuff you were *supposed* to learn in college!

There may be periods in your career when you actually have too much time on your hands. That's right, this is when most Americans surf the Internet, snooze in their office, talk to their significant other on the phone, or double the amount of cigarette breaks throughout the day.

Yet, a go-getter approaches their manager and offers *"You know, I'm all caught-up today. Is there anything you need help with?"* Take initiative on some project or problem in the department, and make sure your boss knows what you are up to. This is your career. You can talk on the phone and take naps after work.

"Treat all of your customers and clients like royalty."

This is another good rule of thumb. Displaying such an attitude should stay with you throughout your career. The emphasis on service

levels has grown dramatically in recent decades. This is what sets organizations apart when product and price are similar in a marketplace.
All of us have had our horror stories of bad service, and consumers
remember bad service well more than they remember good service.
Not only do dissatisfied customers not return, but they tell others not
to buy that product or service either. And without customers or clients,
you don't have a job.

By the way, everyone will have customers or clients in their job.
Most people are familiar with external customers or clients of a company.
However, there is also a constituency referred to as your "internal client,"
which includes fellow employees who may count on your production within
the same company. This is a prominent role played by those who have little
or no interaction with a company's external clients or customers. Examples
include information technology, accounting, and human resources staff.
Quality and satisfaction levels can be measured within this class of
employee, as well. All of your internal and external customers will count
on you for your service, productivity, and professionalism throughout
your career.

"That's not my job."

This is one of the most overused statements in organizations today,
and one of the most hated by managers. Not every single task that
must be done in a company each day can be specifically outlined in an
employee job description. Managers just want to see whatever needs
to be done actually get done--they don't care who does it. So, just do
it. Managers possess a keen memory of who complained about doing
something and who actually did it. Remember this.

Go to your boss with solutions, not just problems. One option is
to just slap a problem on your managers' desk with no background or
warning, and now it is their problem. For example, you can approach
your boss late in the afternoon and say:

> *"There's no way we are going to get those reports finished
> and to our client by tomorrow."*

Or, you can add:

"I just checked with accounting. We should be able to send the finished portions tonight, and send the late portions via e-mail tomorrow afternoon. If that's OK, all we need is your approval."

Some seasoned managers will ask you what the alternatives are or what you recommend should be done about a problem first. This teaches employees to create solutions on their own, and not just dump off problems. Managers have enough problems.

> *Tips on Impressing Your Manager*
> ☺ Volunteer for special projects or committees.
> ☺ Be unselfish and offer to assist other team members.
> ☺ Be willing to stay late and go the extra mile.
> ☺ Treat your customers and clients like royalty.
> ☺ Bring your boss solutions, not just problems.

Lastly, do all the little things, such as cutting out an interesting article you may have read and leaving it in their box with a note, such as:

"Thought you might find this interesting since we've had such a problem with employee turnover. Look what this company in Ohio is doing..."

Managers want to feel you are "in it with them together," and that you are truly on the same team. Ask your boss questions about their career, the direction of the company, and the industry. Such interest and initiative goes a long way. Besides, no one else will be doing it. Those questions help label you as future management material, and you will also be learning, not just trying to look good.

Communicate well with your manager, the good and the bad. You want to form a relationship. Over time, there should be a feeling that you care about them and they care about you. This sounds obvious, but it is rare. Most Americans probably are aware of those extra little things that can lead to advancement in their career, yet millions continue to rush out the door at 4:59 without even saying *"Goodnight."*

Be sincere in your efforts. Don't simply do good things to look good. Experienced managers can distinguish between those who do things for the right reasons, and those who are "brown-nosers." Stay positive, do the right things from the start, and impress the right people. This will help your career stay on the right track through the entire journey.

Recommended Books

Managing Up: 59 Ways to Build a Career-Advancing Relationship with Your Boss
Michael S. Dobson, Deborah Singer Dobson
American Management Association, 1999

Managing Up: How to Forge an Effective Relationship With Those Above You
Rosanne Badowski, Roger Gittines, Jack Welch – Currency, 2003

Managing Your Boss
Sandi Mann – Barron's Educational Series, 2001

The Golden Rule of Schmoozing, Aye Jaye – SourceBooks, 1998

Recommended Seminar

"How to Deliver Exceptional Customer Service"
Fred Pryor Seminars, www.pryor.com, 1-800-556-2998

Your Learning Didn't End, It Is Just Beginning

Successful people make a career out of learning, and continually applying what they learn until they retire. They don't just stop learning at age 22, and neither should you.

It's called personal development. No one is pushing you to learn more. There is no final exam around the corner, and no challenge to raise that "B" to an "A." It's all up to you. This is when self-discipline becomes a factor. Many college graduates are tired of learning, and they're relieved they never have to study anymore. They just want to get a job and that's it.

Be honest with yourself and be aware of gaps you may have in professional knowledge or skills that could slow your advancement. For instance, a major gap most have is giving presentations or public speaking. This is one of the most sought-after skills in the business world today—a skill in which college graduates are often unpolished. Toastmasters is an outstanding organization I became involved in early in my career. I thought it was a tremendous experience. If you simply think *"I don't need to make any speeches in my job,"* that is a short-sighted observation. You must learn how to communicate professionally in a group setting if you expect to move up the ladder.

There is a basic difference between training and development. Training involves skills and knowledge to be applied toward your *current* position, while development involves skills and knowledge to be applied toward *future* positions. Do you want to have future jobs with more responsibility? More responsibility means participation in sales presentations, communication with upper management, further understanding of technical issues, and greater liabilities with financing or budgets. Now, you don't want to wait until you get that position to start being developed for it, do you? And why would someone hire you for those responsibilities to begin with, if you don't already possess those skills? Start developing your skills now to put yourself in position for those positions.

So, what avenues are available to continue your learning? Most larger companies have in-house training and development programs. Be sure your boss is aware that you want to participate in any developmental training that is available. There are also…

☑ *Seminars and other offsite training*
☑ *Conventions, special events, and trade shows*
☑ *Graduate or continuing education courses*
☑ *Trade magazines, newsletters, and websites*
☑ *Non-fiction books*
☑ *Self-help books, tapes, and CD's*
☑ *Peers and colleagues*
☑ *Online/Internet training, or e-learning*

Engage in these resources and activities, and you will be *ahead* of the 8-5 employee sitting to your left who has been in the same position for years, but supposedly knows it all. There's a reason why that person has been there for years. If you are in a seminar or training class, pay attention and take notes *(sound familiar?)*. The information you learn in professional training is much different from that in a college classroom. *It is directly relevant*—so be a sponge.

We are in the age of non-fiction, self-help, and *"101 Ways to Improve"* everything. Because of this demand, there has been a tidal wave of resources in almost every area of life and career, in every field. Very specific trade magazines are available, and most professional associations have their own publication, newsletter, website, or e-zine that provides daily information readers such as you want to know. They include important things, such as the latest trends, how to build your career within the industry, salary information, employment listings, and which companies are growing and which are failing.

Many resources are inexpensive as well, which I'm sure is ideal for the recent college graduate. Some public libraries offer free or low-cost sessions on Microsoft products, light technical skills, and even basic financials. Go to a cheap or used online bookstore and search for great deals in your field or area of interest. You will be surprised how many relevant books you can get for under $5 or $10. Magazines can also be *free* or very inexpensive if you know where to go. Such resources are listed at the end of this chapter. Many companies or organizations you might belong to subscribe to industry magazines, or can offer you discounts, as well.

These books and magazines will look great on your office shelf. And, when you have a spare minute, you just may be inspired enough to grab one and start reading it! The bottom line is, you must be devoted to extra learning in your field. You need the knowledge, and others will be impressed by it. Start learning more now.

If you find it may serve as a benefit some day in your profession, try to become fluent in a foreign language. We continue to rapidly expand into a global economy each year, where such skills are becoming more and more marketable. Depending on the industry, this skill can open doors and create more demand for your services, allowing you to command a higher salary if it is indeed relevant to that position.

Technically Speaking…

Depending on your field, much of what you learned in college classrooms will be out of date within the next five years. Sometimes material is even out of date at the time you are learning it in college, simply because of the slow life cycle of college textbooks. This is due to technology.

Not many industries remain where knowing technology within that industry isn't important. In most industries, you may earn a major advantage over others by capturing technical knowledge as well as industry knowledge. You want there to be a demand for you. Therefore, your skills, talent, and knowledge have to be unique as compared to the average employee.

You don't have to be a computer programmer, but try to understand how electronic transactions or file transfers work. What are the costs, capabilities, and drawbacks of a new technical process or software package as it relates to your department? Always keep abreast of technical trends within your industry and consider taking basic technical courses on the side. Become Internet savvy. Gaining knowledge in these areas can help your career. It helped mine. Most people don't want to understand this stuff. Thus, you can couple your industry knowledge with technical knowledge for a winning, lucrative combination, where employers will seek you out for future positions.

Recommended Books

Seven Habits of Highly Effective People
Stephen R. Covey – Free Press, 1990

Personal Development for Life and Work
Harold R. Wallace, L. Ann Masters
South-Western Educational Publishing, 2000

Act Natural: How to Speak to Any Audience
Ken Howard, Edward Tivnan – Random House, 2003

Recommended Websites

www.life-after-college.com/free-stuff
www.half.com
www.abebooks.com
www.alldiscountbooks.net
www.allbookstores.com

Find A Mentor Within The Company

I remember my first mentor. I was lucky. He was a rising star in a large corporation who, for whatever reason, took an interest in me. He took ten minutes out from his lunch break, or five minutes to stop by after a meeting to chat. And I was all ears.

There are two types of people who will try to tell you about "the way it is" in a company. Unfortunately, many try to place a negative spin on things, and have a narrow view of the big picture. Typically, those are people who are in the same position you are in. Except, they have been there forever. They tell you exactly why you *won't* be successful. The company is unfair, biased, or unappreciative. You will be amazed at how many people are influenced by the naysayers. Forget these people.

Pick someone who is successful and respected by upper management. Pick someone who rose up through the ranks from your position, and someone you admire. Makes sense, doesn't it? Take advice from someone who has succeeded, and they will help you succeed. Some companies sponsor structured mentor programs, as do many professional organizations. Be sure to investigate these options. Otherwise, you will have to rely on a more informal method of finding a mentor.

So, how do you ask someone about giving you advice, or becoming your mentor? Simply approach them. See if you might already have something in common with them (same college, sports, hobby, etc.). You might think these people are too busy, or too important to talk to you. Most times, that is not the case. Deep down, almost everyone relishes having someone "look up to" them. Most people want to share their secrets and their path to success with someone who really wants to listen. And if they were so successful so fast, there is a good chance they have done it the "right way." They value the company and understand they are contributing to its future success by helping to develop other young leaders. Besides, they probably had a mentor, too!

Another avenue is to learn from a professional career coach. Today, people utilize the services of counselors, consultants, therapists, and advisors for just about everything. What could be more valuable than individual, objective advice from a professional for any range of topics in your career?

In an October 19, 2003, *Bankrate.com* article "Career Coach Can Help Sharpen Edge," writer Penelope Trunk states, *"Weaknesses are hard to beat, so if you're really serious about making a personal change, I recommend a career coach."* Trunk added that *"I also learned that when you find a good one, you can change in ways that will surprise you."*

More information on this avenue is provided at:

www.life-after-college.com/coaching

Be Nice To People

Here is a secret to business success you will not learn in any college textbook, but can be one of the most powerful tools you will ever have: Be nice to people.

Do you know how many times you will need favors or assistance from people throughout your career? After thorough research, I have determined my best estimate is somewhere between countless and infinite.

You might think being nice will "soften you up," as this goes against the ruthless corporate philosophy of the 1980's, symbolized by Michael Douglas's character in the movie *Wall Street.* But you can still be a tenacious, ambitious, talented go-getter, *and* be nice to people at the same time. Often, this can be quite a challenge in the pressure-packed world of the corporate environment. It is difficult, but possible!

I have come to completely admire many successful people across several industries who are terrific examples of such a balance. And I can assure you, the balance they display in those areas has been essential to each of them becoming successful in the first place. You will live a much easier life if you develop more friends than enemies. Don't gain a reputation of being a "jerk" or a "bitch." Don't make things hard on yourself. Make things easy.

I have two very successful friends my age that work for the same financial services company. I have never felt that either of them were overwhelmingly skilled at financial analysis or had superior stock market knowledge. However, both of them are two of the nicest people I have ever met. You know these types of people—the ones that everyone seems to like, and there doesn't seem to be a mean bone in their body? They have built up a tremendous base of clientele, mainly due to their personality. It probably helps that they have applied their personality in an industry that is usually identified with the stereotype of dry, dislikable number-crunchers *(sorry accounting and finance majors!)*.

By the way, this certain financial company my friends work for is Edward Jones. Is it a coincidence this company was ranked as Fortune Magazine's *"Best Company to Work For in America"* for 2003? This is the corporate culture and environment that Edward Jones has developed for its employees, and the type of employees it strives to hire and develop. It makes for successful people, successful companies, and satisfied clients.

Don't be afraid to compliment people. Or better yet, ask their advice on things, since they may have more knowledge and experience in an area than you do. That's the ultimate compliment. Get into this habit and you may actually learn more things, too.

Here is only one example of a favor you may need on any given day during your career. Let's assume you have a report that must be changed late in the afternoon and shipped out with a product to your client that day. First, you must run to a computer programmer and ask them to stop what they are doing to help you. They are on a specific schedule of things they are supposed to be working on, and they do not report to you. When you ask them to reprogram a report immediately as a *favor*, they can react in one of two ways:

"Sure, go ahead and give it to me and I'll take care of it for you."

"Why should I do you a favor? Take a number."

Hopefully for your sake, you are greeted with the first response. Thus, if you are fortunate enough to get the report changed by 5:00, you must then run down to shipping where you encounter an hourly employee who leaves every day promptly at....you guessed it....5:00. They have to log back into the system, find your product, and prepare your package for shipping immediately. When you ask them to do this for you as a favor, they can respond in one of two ways:

"Sure, go ahead and give it to me and I'll take care of it for you."

"Why should I do you a favor? I've already clocked out. Goodnight."

Get the picture?

On a larger scale, this can effect internal promotions as well. Hiring managers within the same company do their homework. They could be receiving feedback from someone who only knows your reputation, but not necessarily your work. Managers often have a pretty good eye on what candidate they may want to promote long before it becomes official. They may ask your current manager or others you interact with in the company on a daily basis. Remember, people hire people they like, right? Who wants to work with someone who is known as a jerk?

"Treat others as you would like to be treated."

Treat your peers well, not as competitors to prove yourself against for the next promotion. There is always a chance they will be your next boss. Do favors for people, be a good listener, and take an interest in others. What kind of environment would it be where people only cared about themselves? Being selfish all the time won't get you very far.

Thus far, you have experienced primarily individual study and achievements through college. Many universities have made an emphasis to incorporate more team-related study and projects within their curriculum. This is good. However, for students, they often don't go so well, and who really likes doing them? There are challenges defining responsibility, personality conflicts, and resentment toward those not carrying their weight. Yet, teamwork is the reality of the business world. You have to interact together to get things done.

"What goes around comes around."

Once every three months, leave home 15 minutes early and spend $5.00 on a box of donuts for your office. It's amazing how far $20.00 per year can go, and it should be tax-deductible *(consult your tax attorney for details)*. Whenever you take a jaunt to the vending machine for a beverage, bring an extra 50 cents and ask someone else if they need one, too. This was the most amazing example I remember. I thought it was the greatest thing in the world when someone offered to buy me a soda for no reason. This is what the winners do. And, it only takes a 50-cent investment to make a lasting impression.

Recommended Books

How To Win Friends And Influence People
Dale Carnegie – Pocket, 1990

How to Make People Like You in 90 Seconds or Less
Nicholas Boothman – Workman Publishing, 2000

Talking the Winner's Way: 92 Little Tricks for Big Success in Business and Personal Relationships
Leil Lowndes – McGraw-Hill, 1999

Stay Organized From The Start

Being organized throughout your career will allow management to trust you with greater responsibility. Being disorganized can create a perception with management, such as "How can you manage a department of employees when you can't even manage yourself?"

- *Can you organize your thoughts into spoken word?*
- *Can you organize your ideas into written business communications?*
- *Are you organized enough to make copies of an item to distribute to everyone before a meeting?*
- *Are you organized enough to quickly locate a report you filed somewhere six months ago?*
- *Do you have the ability to coordinate a seamless project with great amounts of material, information, and communication flowing between people?*

You must learn to be clear with expectations, direction, and details in both your verbal and written communication in your career. This is where the majority of mistakes are made, and it usually gets traced back to poor understanding of what was said. Clear follow-ups and recaps are critical to success. Be organized and on top of what steps are to be followed after such conversations or meetings.

Do not have a constantly cluttered desk. It gives the perception that you are sloppy and disorganized. It is also ineffective. You can forget meetings, lose documents, miss deadlines, or make critical mistakes by not being organized. Your first day on the job, create new file folders as needed. Office supplies such as filing cabinets, in/out trays, pin-up boards, desk magnets, and a rolodex are designed to assist professionals in staying organized. But you have to use them—they are not just desk décor.

Keep up on your filing *each day*. File HR notices, company/industry news, magazine or website articles, and all client communications. Compile all the material you gather from every training class and seminar. Take these files and accumulate them from position to position, from job to job, throughout your career.

People will seek you as a resource. It makes you look organized and sincerely interested. Most people trash those items before they even read them. I'm not suggesting you have to read everything. But identify what items may be useful to you in the future, and keep them for when you need to reference them.

Organization skills also relate to your computer files. You will be astonished at how fast the volume of e-mails and electronic documents will pile up on your PC if you do not keep up. Organize and name your electronic file folders and file everything at the end of each day. Otherwise, you will spend valuable time each day asking yourself *"What did I do with last month's accounting report this time?"*

Another thing to remember is: *Write things down*, so you don't have to remember. Although you are young, you will still forget things you think you won't forget. In a fast-paced environment, it is very easy to lose track of one of the hundreds of small tasks you may need to do each day. You might be asked in the hallway to call someone or forward someone an e-mail as soon as possible. The next thing you know, it is the end of the day and you forgot who you were supposed to call or what e-mail you were supposed to send.

Stay organized from the start. It will take you no longer than three minutes at the end of each day to file, straighten up your desk, and create that *"Things to Do"* list for the following day. I still use such a list even today. Thus, leave work at 5:03 instead of 5:00, and you will live an easier life.

Recommended Books

Conquering Chronic Disorganization
Judith Kolberg – Squall Press, 1999

How to Be Organized in Spite of Yourself: Time and Space Management That Works With Your Personal Style
Sunny Schlenger – Signet Books, 1999

Organization Skills (Career Skills Library)
Richard Worth – Ferguson Publishing Company, 1998

Recommended Seminar

"How to Get More Organized"
Padgett-Thompson, www.pttrain.com, 1-800-258-7246

Time Management During Your 20's

On that note, management knows who escapes from work at 4:59 like they are part of the prison release program. They also know who stays late to get that extra responsibility done each night, even if it does cause them to be stuck in traffic. Certainly, your production during those eight hours is most important, but continual sightings after hours can only help the perception of your work ethic. It's sad to say, but staying late creates a perception, and perception is reality. Be willing and available.

This is the area where many college graduates in the workplace begin breaking down. It is a major adjustment to work 40+ hours per week. More than likely, you will be very busy in your 20's. You may get married, have children, buy houses, buy cars, and travel. You will also have to balance work, bills, family obligations, exercise, laundry, etc., on a daily basis. And, of course, you still want to have a social life, correct? That is one full plate.

Yet—these are the years that are most critical in building your career! Leading a healthy, balanced, and enriched life outside of work can make you happier and more productive while you are at work. Invest your time wisely. I never would have survived, let alone succeeded, without meticulous time management during this period. Plan ahead, utilize a daily planner, or even calendar software such as Microsoft Outlook®. At some point, you may even invest in a personal digital assistant (PDA) for yourself.

Don't forget, to be successful you will need to go the extra mile in your career. This could mean working late, joining a professional organization, keeping up on industry news, or perhaps even taking graduate classes at night. Are you willing to make the sacrifices it takes to separate yourself from the pack? If you do make such a commitment, time management skills will be essential.

In college, you didn't brag to your professors about completing your semester project three weeks early. They don't care. Nor did you necessarily care about impressing them. Your grade will be your grade either way.

In the real world, you have to impress people. And, turning in reports or projects three minutes beforehand, or even late—is NOT impressive. Further, as I'm sure you know, procrastination can lead to sloppiness, and even short-cutting items that should have been included in the project. Plan ahead, do a thorough job, and don't place undue stress on yourself. Don't continue to avoid doing tasks you don't like to do, or they will pile up on you.

"Don't wait until the end of your life to stop procrastinating."

Of course, the number one rule of time management is…

Be on time! Don't get the reputation of someone who is late to work, late to meetings, or continuously missing deadlines. It gives the impression you are disorganized, irresponsible, and don't have respect for other employees who are on time. Always return voice mails and e-mails within 24 hours at the latest. These are other items you do not want to pile up on you.

"Work smarter, not necessarily harder."

There is a principle in the business world called "Under-Promise and Over-Deliver." When I first truly discovered what this meant and how to apply it, it was like a revelation. Don't paint yourself into a corner by committing to something you're not sure you can do, simply because that is what someone wants to hear. You are placing overwhelming pressure on yourself, and setting yourself up for failure. Frustration is a function of expectation. Be firm up front and create a realistic expectation for the other party. Now, you have a realistic chance of not only delivering, but exceeding their expectations to look like a hero. Be a hero, not a goat. This principle can be applied to customers, clients, bosses, or other internal departments. It will help keep you from falling behind, and will help to reduce your stress from the start.

If you do feel swamped or overwhelmed, you must communicate that with your manager. Many times, young professionals don't speak up, fearing management may believe they can't handle the job. But you will drown and get burned out otherwise. Good managers will help you prioritize "what must be done now" vs. "what can wait until later." They should also have backup plans and resources available to provide you the help you need, or they should help you themselves. Therefore, make your life easier. Ask for rope to be thrown down *before* you drown!

Recommended Books

Get a Grip! Overcoming Stress and Thriving in the Workplace
Bob Losyk – Wiley Business Trade Books, 2004

The Procrastinator's Handbook: Mastering the Art of Doing It Now
Rita Emmett – Walker & Company, 2000

Getting Things Done: The Art of Stress-Free Productivity
David Allen – Penguin Books, 2003

Recommended Seminars

"Managing Multiple Projects, Objectives, and Deadlines"
Skillpath Seminars, www.skillpath.com, 1-800-677-3200

"Time Management & Organization Skills for Professionals"
National Seminars Group, www.natsem.com, 1-800-258-7246

"Getting it All Done"
Fred Pryor Seminars, www.careertrack.com, 1-800-556-3009

Chapter Five:

Simon Says "Follow the Rules"

Ethics, Honesty, And Integrity

It's amazing how well the strategy of *"keeping your nose clean"* will work throughout your career, as you watch co-workers make mistakes and tumble themselves down the corporate ladder. Who knows, you may earn your first promotion by default! Follow the rules and stay professional at all times. Don't give anyone a reason to collect dirt on you or run you through the rumor mill.

You may not think your managers are that smart, but most of the time, they are smarter than you think. I used to have what I called the *"6th sense of a manager."* I could tell from across the hallway whether my employees were on a personal call or on with a client, just by their tone of voice. If it was a client, I could tell if trouble was in the air, and if so, I would go check on it.

Managers have access to your e-mails, your files, and sometimes your phone conversations. Don't be naïve. You might be able to get away with some things, but you won't get away with everything. And one mistake can be like a grenade explosion on your career path.

The most severe corporate no-no's include fraud, embezzlement, and theft. Awareness of such crimes has escalated in recent years with news stories such as the Enron scandal in 2002. Falsifying documents, inflating financials, and insider trading have severe penalties that often include lengthy prison terms. Unfortunately, we are moving into an era of increasing white-collar crimes, and greed is at the core of the bad apple. Technology, the Internet, and electronic transactions open opportunities for scams and other illegal activity. Yet, resources to crack down on such activities have improved as well, such as the development of high-tech security software and the addition of both internal and external investigative personnel.

According to the U.S. Chamber of Commerce, employee theft costs companies an estimated $20 - $40 billion in losses annually. The chamber also reported that an employee is 15 times more likely to steal from an employer than a non-employee. Now, the most common "minor" thefts include employees taking home pencils, pens, and those irresistible 3M "Post-it®" notes from the supply cabinet.

"That's not really stealing. Everybody does that."

The next level of theft includes extra company shirts, PC accessories, and actual products from inventory your company manufactures.

"Our company's cost on each keyboard mouse is $1.12?
What is $1.12 to a company that made a $100 million last year?"

You've now reached level two. Be especially careful if you are ever tempted to take something from your company's inventory of raw materials or finished product. If your company has even average inventory controls, there are daily or weekly "cycle counts" of each product, a system that tracks when every unit of product was moved and by whom, and video cameras in the warehouse. Part of an inventory manager's job is to be a security guard. These managers are trained to catch people with "sticky fingers" through various methods of investigation.

Another popular practice is the ballooning of expense reports. Taking your friends to lunch, a round of golf, or a sporting event while writing it off on the company may be amusing to you and your friends, but it won't be to the VP of Accounting. Travel expense reports offer another entire world of opportunity for unethical behavior. One example is purchasing a $300 airline ticket on your credit card, submitting the receipt for reimbursement, canceling the reservation, driving the 3½ hours instead, and keeping the $300. There are many tricks to the trade, and they are used every day—surprisingly by people who are otherwise honest and good employees. They often try to rationalize it by defending themselves against themselves:

"My company would be out $300 if I really did fly, so what's the difference?"

"What's another $300 to a $5 billion corporation?"

One final example relates to the world of workers compensation. Let's imagine Stanley is at home doing work in his backyard, and he hurts his back. He decides to struggle to work the next day, trying to hide that he can barely walk. When trying to lift his first box of the day, he drops to the floor in pain, claiming that it's a work-related injury. Six weeks later, he is scheduled to be fit to return, but he fakes additional pain in his back to get another four weeks off work from the doctor. This example is called *taking advantage of the system*. It's also called fraud, and it costs Stanley's company thousands of dollars in workers compensation costs and lost productivity. It is also punishable by law, up to and including prison time.

Besides being illegal, these examples fall into the framework of ethics, honesty, and integrity. There are also instances of directly lying or misleading a customer to get a sale. Most of us have our own stories of being the victim as a customer at some point. How did you feel about that salesperson? How did you feel about that company?

Lying to your boss to stay out of trouble, or to not take ownership of a critical mistake that was made, is never a good idea. Once your boss loses trust in you, you can forget about being promoted anywhere in the company. Again, most bosses understand and accept that employees will make mistakes. They will respect honesty, and will turn their focus to simply making sure the same mistake doesn't happen again in the future. They don't respect lying, nor will they accept it.

The bottom line is be careful, someone may be watching you. There really is a slippery slope in this environment, so don't start slipping. The repercussions may be more than just losing one job. Try explaining your reasons for discharge in your next interview, and see if that impresses the hiring manager. These things ruin careers. DON'T RISK IT!

Recommended Books

Making Good: How Young People Cope with Moral Dilemmas at Work
Wendy Fischman, Becca Solomon, Howard Gardner, Deborah Greenspan
Harvard University Press, 2004

Ethics in the Workplace: A Systems Perspective
William F. Roth – Prentice Hall, 2004

Integrity Matters,
James F. Bracher, Daniel E. Halloran – Torchlight Publishing, 2004

Recommended Website

www.business-ethics.com

E-mail And The Internet: Etiquette, Use, And Abuse

Don't surf pornographic sites. Don't open e-mails with inappropriate content. Don't send and receive personal e-mails from your work PC during work hours. Lastly, don't be the moron who opens an unknown attachment and spreads a deadly computer virus throughout every PC in your company. It only takes one click, so don't be tempted!

Also, proofread and double check the name of the person(s) to whom you are sending the e-mail. In larger companies, there may be Becky Watson, Bob Watson, Brenda Watson, etc. Don't embarrass yourself. Don't click "Reply All" on a mass e-mail, when your intent was to just respond back to the sender. But instead, you just sent the comment *"Man, I'm so hung over"* to 2,372 employees on your company's e-mail list.

If you think these issues fall into the obvious category, then why do so many American workers damage their career each year by such stupidity? According to the January 2004 issue of *Entrepreneur* magazine, two-thirds of HR professionals have discovered porn on employee computers, and 92% of managers monitor employees' use of the Internet and e-mail.

I had one employee who was caught surfing a pornographic site on his lunch hour. This was against company policy, and he was warned. The following week, he was caught surfing the same pornographic website. This time, he was vehemently warned, told that his PC was under constant monitoring, and that he would be fired for any other violation. The following week, he did it again and was fired.

I had another employee at a different company get warned for excessive e-mail use. She had averaged over 100 personal e-mails sent *per hour*, and of course, her work quality and production were slumping badly. She abstained for about three weeks, then resumed excessive use, even after being told she was being monitored. She was fired.

These stories are not unusual. In fact, they are in the tens of thousands every year. *The New York Times* fired 23 employees in 1999 for circulating an e-mail porn message. In 2000, Dow Chemical fired over 40 employees, and disciplined over 400 more, for inappropriate e-mail use. Companies are becoming even more aware of the severity of the problem, thus strict policies are being written and enforced. And, as mentioned, the technology in security and investigative software to monitor such misuse is much improved and accessible. In other words, you can't run and you can't hide anymore, so just don't do it.

Stay out of the habit of forwarding jokes via e-mail. It can become an addiction. Just because *"Bob and Sally send jokes back and forth to their friends, and nobody says anything to them,"* doesn't mean it is wise for you to. Tell your friends to send jokes or attachments to a separate, personal e-mail address that you can check from your home. Your work e-mail should be for work e-mail. Your job is to impress your bosses and work hard for your company, and you can't do that sending personal e-mails and surfing the Internet.

E-mail does have a very practical application in the workplace. It is a tremendous tool. E-mail allows someone to instantly provide detailed information to a group of readers in a variety of locations. It provides the ability to attach reports, documents, pictures, video clips, and website links. Over-dependency on using e-mail for everything throughout the day does tend to develop poor habits, and can erode personal and professional communication skills. Too often e-mail takes the place of walking 15 feet down the hallway to interact with another human being. E-mail shouldn't serve as an emotional outlet for you to vent anger about an issue, and you should never use e-mail to resolve personal differences with a fellow employee. That is a face-to-face human function.

E-mails are intended to be short communication messages. If your message is longer than what fits on the readers' screen, the reader will most likely not read it all, or just lightly skim as they scroll down. Be clear, and even thorough, but be concise. Be sure to proofread your e-mails before you send, *especially* if management will be receiving them. Carbon-copy (cc:) your bosses on pertinent e-mails, or even messages that update them on the good work you are doing. If someone makes a minor mistake on the job, don't carbon-copy (cc:) their boss on an e-mail to get them in trouble. People do not like that. One other cardinal rule is not to TYPE USING CAPITAL LETTERS BECAUSE IT GIVES THE READER THE IMPRESSION YOU ARE SCREAMING.

There are many other e-mail communication tips outlined in the resources section. As with many other lessons in the business world, common sense and professionalism should ultimately prevail.

Recommended Books

E-Mail Etiquette: Do's, Don'ts and Disaster Tales from People Magazine's Internet Manners Expert
Samantha Miller – Warner Books, 2001

E Writing: 21st Century Tools for Effective Communication
Dianna Booher – Pocket, 2001

Business E-Mail: How to Make It Professional and Effective
Lisa A. Smith – Writing & Editing, 2001

Drugs, Alcohol, And Your Career

Periodically, we watch the news and learn the lesson of someone famous ruining a career or life with drug or alcohol use. Often it is an athlete or entertainer. But we don't necessarily equate that to the corporate world. Drug and alcohol use can badly affect job performance, severely damage your reputation, create nasty rumors, cause you to be passed over for promotions, or even worse, lead to criminal conviction. Although this has not been mentioned yet, jail time is one of the biggest barriers to building a successful career.

Attention: *This is serious now.* If you have engaged in drug use in the past, stop. If you haven't in the past—don't be tempted to start. Not that there is ever a smart time in your life to use drugs, but using them when starting your career is the worst timing you can have. Besides, drug testing at the time of employment has become much more prevalent in companies today, and you should be provided with a strict company policy on drug and alcohol use upon hiring.

According to the National Institute for Mental Health, 73 percent of drug users are employed, and 8 million workers abuse drugs. Some 79 percent of *Fortune 1000* CEO's rated addiction as a significant problem for their companies. It affects productivity, morale, absenteeism, safety, and disability costs. If you or a fellow employee has a problem, there are avenues for help. Most companies subscribe to some type of employee assistance program (EAP's) for individuals struggling with such problems. If not, there are numerous public programs that should be available in your area.

Here is a repeat of an earlier lesson. Managers are just a little smarter than you give them credit for. Do not assume they don't know who is on drugs and who is not. More than likely, they have seen this before. And rumors spread like wildfire within a company—*don't ever underestimate this.* Rumors can almost be worse than a guilty verdict in the professional world, as perception is reality.

The age when a person enters the workforce is eerily close to the age when it is legal for them to start drinking. This is not a good combination. Bill Cosby in the movie *Bill Cosby: Himself* performed a great skit about working hard during the week, drinking too much, and getting sick. *"You give them Saturday and Sunday off, and they work so hard to get to those two days, and those are the days they totally destroy themselves."*

Fun, isn't it? Now, that is an example of the weekend partier. Unfortunately, too many recent college graduates still can't discriminate over which day of the week it is when they drink too much. Limit the amount of weeknights you go out and "paint the town red," and drink in moderation. Don't go to work hung over. You must give your career your best effort, and you can't do that when you are not at your best. Coming in late, tired, and hung over may impress co-workers who think you are cool, but it won't impress your boss.

At some point, you will finally learn that this is stupid. It is just a question of what age you learn this lesson, and how much damage you have caused by then. This issue is often simply a choice all graduates must make about their lifestyle. Commitment, dedication, and self-discipline are what determine the winners from losers in this area.

Don't get me wrong. I had a blast in my 20's. I went out with friends, went to concerts, attended sporting events, and traveled to exotic places. Yet, I always kept a strong sense of priorities and balance. I skipped countless happy hours with my friends when I was studying for evening graduate classes, or when I knew I needed to work late. I thank myself now for the priorities and self-discipline I had when I was younger. You will thank yourself, too.

Recommended Books

Kill the Craving: How to Kill the Impulse to Use Drugs and Alcohol
Joseph Santoro Ph.D. – New Harbinger Publications, 2001

Working Clean and Sober: A Guide for All Recovering People
David Skibbins Ph.D.
Hazelden Publishing & Educational Services, 2000

Recommended Other

Alcohol Treatment Referral Hotline
1-800-252-6465 *or* www.adcare.com

Alcohol and Drug Information-Prevention Online
www.health.org

National Drug and Alcohol Line
1-800-662-HELP (4357)

Smokers Be Aware, Or Beware

What Smoke Signals Are You Giving?

The most recent estimates show that between 25%-35% of college students smoke, or 3-4 million students. Relax, I am not going to try to convince you of all the reasons to quit (time, money, health, smell, perception, etc.); that would take another entire book. However, there are a few key points to make in regard to smoking and your career.

It's important to consider the perception of smoking in a professional workplace, especially if you do indeed enter a "white-collar" environment. Studies have found that 37 percent of blue-collar men and 33 percent of blue-collar women smoke, as compared to 21 percent of men and 20 percent of women in white-collar professions. According to study author Glorian Sorensen, director of the Center for Community-based Research at the Dana Farber Cancer Institute in Boston, smoking rates are dropping faster for white-collar workers than for blue-collar employees, and white-collar workers reported that smoking was becoming less acceptable at work.

More and more executives are understanding the impact smoking has on lost productivity, sick days, rising health insurance costs, and morale issues with their non-smoking co-workers. Many may also question the rational decision-making abilities of those who smoke.

In most companies, there are no set rules for time allotted to smoke or number of smoke breaks allowed throughout the day. Therefore, it is up to the *judgment* of each individual. It is sad to say, but be aware if your boss or company managers are smokers. If they are, you can probably get away with plenty of smoke breaks and it won't be an issue. In fact, it could even be argued that smoke breaks are one of those informal opportunities to get to know bosses and managers even better on a personal level, which can always help your career. (NOTE to non-smokers: *Do not decide to start smoking because of this opportunity!*)

However, if your boss and management are not smokers, be aware. They may not have a policy, or may not ever mention anything to you, but they know. Trust me, they know. I recall once having a conversation with our Operations Manager, who was also a non-smoker. We closed the door and calculated how many labor hours and how much produc-tivity was lost by smoke breaks throughout the day. We tracked the number of smoke breaks, and the amount of time spent from the second they left their desk until the second they returned and actually became productive again. This included putting on their coat (if needed), rallying the troops (stopping by each office to recruit other smokers to join), a trip down in the elevator, etc. You get the picture.

We concluded *(somewhat half-heartedly)* that non-smokers should receive an extra 5 weeks of vacation per year over smokers. Based on an average of 12 minutes wasted per smoke break, multiplied by an average of four smoke breaks per day, it equals an average of 48 minutes of unproductive time per employee per day.

Annualized, this means:

$$48 \text{ minutes per day } =$$
$$4 \text{ hours per week } =$$
$$208 \text{ hours per year } =$$
$$5.2 \text{ weeks per year!}$$

So, just because *"Dan and Sally take eight smoke breaks a day, and nobody says anything to them,"* that is not a good reason for you to take eight also. Remember, your job is to impress your bosses and do the best job you can for your company. You can't do that standing outside in the parking lot puffing away.

Recommended Books

Kicking Butts: Quit Smoking and Take Charge of Your Health
American Cancer Society, 2002

American Lung Association 7 Steps to a Smoke-Free Life
Edwin B. Fisher – Wiley, 1998

Workplace Wellness: The Key to Higher Productivity and Lower Health Costs
Carol Bayly-Grant, Robert E. Brisbin – Wiley, 1997

Recommended Websites

www.americanheart.org   www.hhs.gov/safety   www.ash.org

Avoiding Bad News With Performance Reviews

What does a performance review look like? Most employees don't find out until 6 or 12 months after they begin and are being reviewed for the first time. Ask up front what your performance will be judged on, what the standards and expectations are, and how raises and promotions are determined. Similar to a course syllabus, you need to know exactly what you will be graded on, correct?

It's always important for you to know what areas you are doing well in, what areas you need to improve on, and how you can continue to develop your skills. Most companies are not very good at this process, unfortunately. Clients, projects, pressures, and responsibilities consume the thoughts and energies of everyone every day. Thus, periodically ask your manager for this feedback, as opposed to waiting for a surprise at performance review time.

Every company also has some type of employee handbook, or a thick publication of company policies, regulations, and procedures. Typically, someone will hand you a three-ring binder your first day, blow the dust off, and say, *"Read this."* They will then make you sign that you read it and acknowledge its contents. From there on, you are accountable. You may want to skim through and read the sections that just might pertain to you some day.

Certainly, all companies have policies on the major violations already discussed in this chapter. But, there are hundreds of other rules to be followed within every company and every industry. Try to learn which specific issues your company or manager considers particularly important. These issues may be listed in bold letters on memo after memo, or even posted on company bulletin boards. You just may have to ask your manager, or other experienced employees, about rules people have been previously reprimanded for violating.

There are many infractions an employee may be cited for in everyday work life. This may occur during performance review time, or during immediate and more formal action, if necessary.

The laundry list of potential infractions to avoid includes:

Performance Related

☒ Not meeting set performance standards.

☒ Not following procedure as trained or instructed.

☒ Producing sloppy or inaccurate work.

☒ Committing a major mistake, or a pattern of the same mistakes.

☒ Not producing output in a timely fashion, or not meeting deadlines.

☒ Not obtaining prior approval for a purchase or action.

☒ Exceeding budget guidelines or expense allowances; misuse of company funds.

☒ Manipulating the system, going around the system, taking advantage of the system, or abusing the system.

Behavior Related

☹ Disagreeing with or criticizing management decisions.

☹ Not working independently; needing constant supervision.

☹ Refusing to work with others; displaying poor teamwork.

☹ Having personality conflicts with others.

☹ Allowing personal problems to affect performance.

☹ Unwilling/resistance to change.

☹ Misusing company time; conducting personal business on company time and resources.

☹ Being tardy, taking long lunches, abusing sick day policies.

☹ Insubordination, cursing, backstabbing, complaining, undermining, gossiping, lying, making excuses, finger-pointing, dishonesty, possessing an overall bad attitude, and displaying a general lack of professionalism.

Unlike at Al's Pizzeria, where Al will either yell at you at the top of his lungs, or just fire you on the spot, there are processes that must be followed for employee discipline in the business world. Violation of such policies could lead to disciplinary action by management or the human resources manager. Being sent to the HR manager's office is a bit like being sent to the principal's office in grade school, except the stakes are much higher and the penalties are more severe. Find yourself getting corporate detentions, and you will find yourself never getting corporate promotions.

There are many formal methods and formats for employee discipline. They typically may include:

- ☒ Verbal warning
- ☒ Written warning
- ☒ 2nd written warning
- ☒ 30-60-90 day follow-up reviews
- ☒ Suspension with pay
- ☒ Suspension without pay
- ☒ Termination

Take notice: *All of these steps do not mean that you have nine lives!*

Besides, there are other informal negative consequences or repercussions your boss may either consciously or subconsciously inflict:

- ☹ No raise or low percentage raise
- ☹ No recommendations for promotion
- ☹ Unwanted, poor, or less prestigious assignments
- ☹ Difficult, tedious, or time-consuming extra projects
- ☹ Spreading your actions/reputation to higher members of management

Internal promotions are critical opportunities for advancement throughout your career. Hiring managers from within the company will look at your employee file, especially your performance reviews, before considering promotion. Therefore, these can be damaging actions, unless a consistent pattern of improvement can be established afterwards.

So, why are such formal courses of action taken instead of managers just "pulling someone aside and talking to them"? There are several motivations from a management perspective. Sometimes action by management is necessary to prove to a client, or internal employees, that *"something is being done—action is being taken"* about a particular problem. It could be an attempt by managers to cover their bases, either legally or from an accountability standpoint with upper management on issues such as safety, sexual harassment, confidentiality, etc. It may also start the documentation or paper trail that sets the groundwork for further action or termination of the employee.

If you are in error and are disciplined for any of these issues, accept responsibility for your actions. Apologize, be sincere, and follow any corrective action that may be needed to ensure it doesn't happen again. Most performance-related issues should include some type of performance-improvement plan by your manager, which may involve additional training or assistance from a fellow employee.

Managers don't want to deal with these headaches. Having to discipline an employee is not an enjoyable part of their job. It is also counterproductive to both manager and employee in regard to the time and paperwork the process takes, while real work needs to get done. This is why many managers let things slide, or try to handle them informally, until the problem starts to get out of control.

Managers want to see the problem turned around. They made a decision to hire you. They take pride in believing they hired the right person. And, there were costs involved to recruit and train you. They want you to succeed. Besides, when a manager's employees succeed, the manager succeeds. Remember, both manager and employee should be working together on the same team.

Chapter Six:

Formal Advice
for Informal Situations

Office Politics: An Everyday Campaign

The presence of office politics is a reality. Perhaps in an ideal world, success should be determined strictly on job performance. But, this is the real world, and success is derived from a variety of other factors. If you not only accept these factors, but capitalize on their opportunities, you can elevate your career to higher levels than your skills alone might take you. On the other hand, failure to "play the game" can result in an unhappy, stagnant career in which you accumulate more enemies than friends.

Some basic principles of human behavior exist at the basic root of office politics. The desire for social acceptance goes back to kindergarten, and it doesn't end when you enter the working world. In fact, it continues to evolve.

> ! People want to be liked.
> ! People want to be accepted by their peers.
> ! People want to feel that they are part of a group.
> ! People want their voice to be heard.
> ! People want their voice to influence others.
> ! People want to be included in the latest gossip.
> ! People want to be invited to informal social gatherings.
> ! People want to try to impress the boss.

In addition to these inherent wants and needs, there are great differences within employees in how they exert these wants and needs. Employees come from all educational, geographical, and religious backgrounds. There is also a great mix of age, race, gender, and personality types within every organization. Combine such diversity with the pressures of a 40+ hour work week, and there are plenty of opportunities for the melting pot to boil over.

You may not be destined to get along with every fellow employee, but you need to be determined to work and function together as a team. Because, ultimately, you are on the same team as your co-workers, ideally striving toward the same company goals. Many find dealing with office politics and understanding corporate culture the most challenging aspect of their career.

This is related to the concept of possessing "emotional intelligence," or "EQ," in the workplace. This involves the ability to understand the emotions of yourself and others effectively, and applying that understanding using interpersonal skills. Many major corporations, as well as the U.S. military, have provided emotional intelligence training for their employees, managers, and leaders. Unofficially, approximately 99.99% of all employees have some form of interaction with other human beings in their job. Therefore, these skills are important, as you will encounter different interpersonal situations with different personality types every day of your career.

Examples of different work personality types include a socializer, an introvert, an egomaniac, a know-it-all, a brown-noser, a workaholic, and a "bare minimum to get by" guy, just to name a few. There are also unspoken roles or positions of people within an organization that can be important to recognize. Even though certain individuals may not be labeled with different titles, there are those who are leaders and opinion-molders nonetheless.

Perhaps these people have been in the company or position for several years, have more training and knowledge than others, and have close contacts with upper management. These individuals may also have strong personalities and an informal following of others. If you don't include them on a suggestion you got approved, you may hear a shriek coming from across the office one day, and the outburst:

"Whose bright idea is this?
This is going to take us an extra 10 hours to do every week!"

If you check with these people first instead, they will appreciate the advanced solicitation of feedback. They may tell you that the company has already tried that idea in the past and explain to you why it didn't work. This feedback may even save you the embarrassment of bringing a bad idea to your manager beforehand, or at least being aware of the potential negatives to the idea.

However, also be careful to follow processes and be aware of the proper channels present within your organization. You may encounter managers who make decisions you don't like, change your job responsibilities, or take credit for your work. Perhaps you feel you never get noticed, appreciated, or thanked. Perhaps they are always criticizing and negative toward you, but they compliment and favor others. If any of these issues arise, you just can't go to your boss's boss and start complaining. You must try to work with your managers, not go over their head.

Managers often see things from an entirely different perspective. When you have established a rapport and relationship with your manager, you can certainly inquire about why they did what they did, and perhaps they can provide you with more insight on their actions that you may not have considered. Those discussions may help you develop managerial skills for the future.

"That's not fair. I work harder than they do."

This common situation may be considered the "tattletale dilemma." There may be occasions where you will be challenged with what you perceive as unfairness between yourself and other employees. You think it should be brought to management's attention, but you don't want to "rock the boat" and be considered a tattletale, because that can result in that person and everyone else in the office hating you. Such examples may include an employee who:

- ☺ Gets paid more than you, but doesn't work as hard.
- ☺ Always surfs the Internet and sends personal e-mails.
- ☺ You continually have to cover for, or help do their work.
- ☺ Arrives late, takes long lunches and frequent smoke breaks, and leaves early.
- ☺ Always shortcuts reports or projects.
- ☺ Continually breaks a rule, gets around the rules, or cheats.
- ☺ Makes mistakes, but is able to "bury them" so no one will find out.

Perhaps one employee falls into the "tattletale" categories above, but still gets the best reviews and the highest raises. This could be due to professional favoritism, which some refer to as the business equivalent of a "teacher's pet." Nepotism is another similar form of favoritism. You will experience instances of father-son, brother-sister, and especially husband-wife combinations that affect the workplace. The additional influences of physical/dating relationships with the workplace will be addressed later in this chapter. Each of these examples results in resentment, jealousy, low morale, and ultimately poor team performance.

Other Common Situations Where Office Politics Arise

- ❗ Raises or promotions earned for other reasons than merit.
- ❗ Cliques of a few that exclude many; popularity contests.
- ❗ Preferential treatment because an employee is attractive.
- ❗ Everyone trying to get on the good side of a new manager.
- ❗ Dealing with layoffs or firings of friends/co-workers.
- ❗ People who talk behind people's back.
- ❗ Dealing with changes in responsibility.
- ❗ Business decisions based on personal motives.
- ❗ Conflicts between employees and management.

Conflicts between managers and employees have existed since prehistoric times. Unfortunately, not all managers are liked, agreed with, or even respected by their employees. There may be several disgruntled employees verbally abusing your manager behind their back and refusing to adhere to instruction. You may be stuck between doing what your manager instructs you to do and what the rest of the group actually does.

In situations like these, it is easy to *say* you will do the right thing, but the pull to just go along with the group can be strong. As in high school, a type of peer pressure is present, which stems from the desire for social acceptance. Another example of this situation is being caught in the middle of a personality conflict between two co-workers:

> *"Can you believe that jerk? He is the worst excuse ever for a project manager, don't you think?"*
> Then they turn to you for your agreement.
> *"Ummm...yeah...he sure is."*
> You just gave in to office politic peer pressure.

If you get in a pattern of taking strong stands against individuals, you will paint yourself into a corner within one year, and have virtually nobody left on *your* side. Such "counter-networking" can make life difficult in that position, and can even follow you to future positions. It's a small world. Future employers will call someone they know at your current company and ask what they know about you. Hopefully, incorrectly handling people and situations won't hurt you too badly in that regard.

So, how should you deal with all of these issues?

Whenever possible, don't take personal sides. Be diplomatic. Consider saying *"You both have good points,"* or *"Why don't you just go talk to him about it?"* That's not taking sides. In fact, that's rational and professional advice. It's called tact, discipline, common sense, and keeping focus on what is best for you and your career. In each situation, also consider what is in the best interest of the company. That is always another safe and objective way to view things.

It is OK to show some backbone and voice your opinion. Voice it positively and professionally, without taking shots at others, and people will respect that. So speak up, especially if you know you are standing up for something that is right. If you do not voice your opinion, you may be walked on your entire career, and risk not being considered a tough decision-maker or stand-up person. You will learn to use discretion and judgment, and learn to "pick your battles" as you become more experienced.

Will enduring such issues make you want to leave that company? Hopefully, not. If you are in a bad situation nearing your last straw, address the issue head on, and be patient enough for the problem to change or improve. It could be that management, or the other employees, aren't actually aware that the problem is so severe. Sometimes people don't *intend* for their actions to be damaging. They may just be acting naturally and are oblivious to the impacts of their actions. Generally speaking, most managers at least attempt to be fair, and generally speaking, most who earn promotions and win awards actually do have the merit to back them up.

Don't be too uptight about all these extra-curricular concerns. You do have a job to perform—a job you can ideally enjoy each day. Smile, joke, laugh, and try to be a generally likable person who gets along with everyone. Assist others when needed and be a good teammate. That will win you over more acceptance than fake, insincere politick-ing. Always consider what might be a win-win situation in a dilemma, and apply the WIIFM principle of what others may desire: *"What's in it for me?"*

Employees are not robots. Employees are people. They have emotions, frustrations, family problems, health issues, good days, and bad days. People become jealous or hurt when things don't go their way. People become angered or unmotivated when they believe they have suffered an injustice. People want to make more money and wriggle their way into the next promotion. You have to accept and understand all of these realities within the working world. Be a winner in the game of office politics, not a loser. Many people are losers for 5-10 years before they figure it out, and others never figure it out.

Recommended Books

People Styles at Work: Making Bad Relationships Good, and Good Relationships Better
Robert Bolton, Dorothy Grover Bolton – Amacom, 1996

A Survival Guide to Working With Humans: Dealing with Whiners, Backstabbers, Know-it-Alls, and Other Difficult People
Gini Graham Scott, PhD. – Amacom, 2004

The EQ Difference: A Powerful Plan for Putting Emotional Intelligence to Work
Adele Lynn – Amacom, 2004

Type Talk at Work (Revised): How the 16 Personality Types Determine Your Success on the Job
Otto Kroeger, Janet M. Thuesen, Hile Rutledge – Delta, 2002

Work Would Be Great If It Weren't for the People: Making Office Politics Work For You
Ronna Lichtenberg – Hyperion, 1999

The 17 Essential Qualities of a Team Player: Becoming The Kind of Person Every Team Wants
John C. Maxwell – Nelson Books, 2002

Recommended Seminars

"Dealing with Difficult People"
Fred Pryor Seminars, www.careertrack.com, 1-800-556-3009

"Strengthening Your People Skills in the Workplace"
National Seminars Group, www.natsem.com, 1-800-258-7246

"How to Handle People with Tact and Skill"
Fred Pryor Seminars, www.careertrack.com, 1-800-556-3009

"Conflict Management and Confrontational Skills"
Fred Pryor Seminars, www.careertrack.com, 1-800-556-3009

Recommended Website

www.officepolitics.com

The Social Side Of The Company Environment

Social environments in the professional world may include functions such as a client dinner, an employee happy hour, a holiday party, a concert, a sporting event, or a charity golf tournament. *(Yes, learn to play golf now if you don't know already!)* Other examples may simply include lunch with a co-worker, "water cooler talk," or other informal gatherings where non-business-related conversations take place.

You should get to know everyone you can in your company on a personal basis. This includes people above you, below you, or in the same position as you. Try to remember at least one key thing about each person you mingle with for future reference. Talk about hobbies, family, travel, etc. Be safe and try to avoid politics whenever possible. No matter what your stance is on any issue, 50% of everyone else disagrees with you, and unfortunately that does cause conflict. There are enough opportunities for conflict within normal business operations.

Try to expand your horizons both personally and professionally. You never know when you will get caught in a conversation you wish you could engage in or at least avoid sounding stupid. Even if you don't like sports, try to read the sports page at least once a week, or even once a month, to stay familiar with popular players or local teams. The same goes for books, movies, politics, or even industry news. Just the basics will do. Being able to relate to and socialize with others of vastly different interests can really come in handy throughout your career. You may just grow as a person, as well.

One important area to understand and exercise is dinner etiquette. If your idea of etiquette is offering the last piece of leftover pizza to your cohort before you give it to your dog, you've got a ways to go. You may just need a crash course before your career even starts, as many interviews are conducted over lunch or dinner meetings. Fortunately, many larger companies offer such etiquette programs to employees as part of their training and development curriculum. If that isn't available, there should be off-site programs within your area, or other resources you can refer to for assistance.

When at a restaurant in a professional setting, don't order the most expensive item on the menu, unless the buyer specifically invites you to do so. Don't order an alcoholic beverage unless the other party does, or the other party explicitly states that is OK. Understand what utensils to use with what courses. Be cognizant of posture, pace, and basic table manners, and know exactly how the bill will be handled. There are so many rules to follow, and you need to become comfortable with all of them. Try taking an interest in learning at least the basics of wine, as well. Remember the importance of portraying the image of management material in this area. Don't embarrass yourself.

Often, corporate functions transpire outside normal working hours. Many view these functions as optional, and feel they impose on their schedule. *"No one can make me go because it doesn't fall in between the hours of 8-5."* That mindset is foolish and backwards. You should always want to attend social functions whenever possible, and view them as an opportunity to help your career.

It is OK to mix in a little work with the conversation at social functions, but not too much. Don't bore someone who deals with work problems 40+ hours per week, and is trying to enjoy themselves for a night. Always speak with bosses or management, but only speak briefly—less than 10 minutes. Don't look like a "boss hog" or too much of a brown-noser. Nobody likes a brown-noser, not even the bosses.

Never behave badly, or say something you will regret the next day at work. *Tip:* It is much more difficult to control yourself if inebriated. Again, this is where self-discipline becomes a factor. If you do drink socially at such an event, drink under control. Be aware of how much your managers are drinking, and what their topics of conversation are. If you are suave, you may just catch that brief window of opportunity to get the break you need.

"Oh, so you like golf, too…" your VP chuckles, downing another martini. *"Remind me, and the next time our client is in, I'll take you to the Club with us."*

You just went up two rungs on the promotion ladder.

Certainly, it's not always quite that easy. However, you will be amazed at how much the social side of business can impact your career path. You have a better chance of getting those big breaks by "hobnobbing" than by reading every career book you can get your hands on.

It seems that social functions in the company environment have been getting toned-down in the last 15 years. There is a crackdown on what activities companies spend their money on and a rise in risk-management issues when alcohol is involved. If you find these opportunities are limited in your company, ask different people to lunch each week. It doesn't even have to be members of management; it could simply be peers who may have different job responsibilities than you. Learn what they do and get to know them. Knowledge is power. And the more you know about how the whole operation works, the easier that enables you to reach management some day.

By taking part in formal social functions, as well as informal social conversations, you will be helping your future career track. You will also discover how much easier it is to get things done in the office when you have a personal relationship with co-workers. And don't forget to be nice to people.

Recommended Books

The Etiquette Advantage in Business:
Personal Skills for Professional Success
Peggy Post, Peter Post – Harper Resource, 1999

Power Etiquette: What You Don't Know Can Kill Your Career
Dana May Casperson – American Management Association, 1999

How to Work a Room: The Ultimate Guide to Savvy Socializing
in Person and Online
Susan RoAne – Harper Collins, 2000

Dress For Success: Casual Day Does Not Mean Be A Slob Day

"Dress for the job you want, not for the job you have."

"It is always better to over-dress than under-dress."

These are both wise sayings to follow. Look sharp at all times. Your professional image and future is at stake every day. Look around the office each day. You should be one of the best-dressed individuals in your position. If you say you do not have the money to spend on nice work clothes, spend less money on something else in your life and sacrifice, because this is important. Consider it an investment.

I have heard, and even concurred at times with such labeling as, "Yeah, they work hard, I'm just not so sure they are *management material.*" This has to do with professionalism and image. For right or wrong, it has kept many from moving up the corporate ladder, or at least slowed them down. Have the image of a star. Don't fall into the trap of "*It must be OK to wear a warm-up outfit on casual day, because other people do too.*" Your goal is to be *better* than everyone else.

One good tip I heard *(but never practiced)* was to keep a nice white shirt in your car at all times, in case you spill something on the shirt you are wearing that day. There are several tremendous resources for formal and casual business dress tips, specific to both men and women, in the resources section.

The basics...

- ☑ Always have your clothes ironed or dry-cleaned.
- ☑ Wear clean and polished dress shoes.
- ☑ Be color-coordinated.
- ☑ Have some sense of style or fashion.
- ☑ Have a professional appearance (hair, makeup, jewelry).
- ☑ Show no visible body piercing or tattoos.
- ☑ Look nice, but not too sexy or provocative.
- ☑ Tuck in your shirt.
- ☑ Don't forget your belt.

According to human resources consulting firm William M. Mercer, 90% of firms interviewed in a 2000 survey offer some form of casual dress code. Nearly two-thirds have casual dress year-round, with the rest limiting it to certain days of the week, typically Fridays, or the summer. These policies DO NOT MEAN you can wear whatever you want.

Many companies have gone backwards and abandoned casual dress privileges because of slobs who abused the policy. Don't be one of those slobs. Brand alcohol beach party shirts, spandex, baseball caps, flip-flops, tank tops, and sunglasses should not be worn to work, even on casual Fridays. When getting dressed, always consider what the people deciding on your next promotion might think if they were judging your outfit, *because they will be.*

Recommended Books

Beyond Business Casual:
What to Wear to Work If You Want to Get Ahead
Ann Marie Sabath – Career PR, 2000

Chic Simple Dress Smart for Men:
Wardrobes that Win in the Workplace
Kim Johnson Gross, Jeff Stone – Warner Books, 2002

Chic Simple Dress Smart for Women:
Wardrobes that Win in the Workplace
Kim Johnson Gross, Jeff Stone – Warner Books, 2002

Recommended Website

www.dressforsuccess.org

Dating In The Workplace: Is It Really Worth It?

OK, so maybe I'm the last person who should be giving advice on dating, but *trust me on this one!* Dating someone you work with is not a great idea. If you are living in a city with 1 million residents, and you are working for a company with 500 employees, use that pool of 999,500 people *outside* your company for your prospective dating partners.

The attractive co-worker in the cubicle to your left is not a fellow classmate. Passing notes, sending e-mails, or relentless flirting may seem innocent at the time, but could lead to disaster. You have too much to lose.

Unfortunately, work can be an enticing environment. You will spend considerably more time at work with the opposite sex than you will in any other environment. And, of course, since you will be dressing your best at work, that may cause people to be looking at you—for reasons other than just that next promotion. There are many social conversations within the work environment, such as the Monday morning storytelling about exciting weekends and the Friday afternoon previews of exciting weekends. This is a natural lead into *"So, what are you doing this Saturday night?"*

Let's explore some of the disincentives of beginning a relationship in the workplace. Your thoughts, energies, and emotions drift to other things than just your job responsibilities. Dating someone in the office threatens a drop in job performance, impairs professional judgment, and leads to excessive e-mail, phone, or personal conversations. So, you think you can try to keep your relationship secret from everyone to avoid problems? Ha....*No one has ever pulled that off!* The rumors will defeat you.

Perhaps the most damaging part of a work relationship is *after the break-up.* This can get ugly, embarrassing, and uncomfortable, while creating irrevocable damage to your reputation through the gossip airwaves. All of the gory and intimate details are funneled throughout your building, almost immediately. People from other departments, including some you have never met, either scowl or giggle at you in the hallway. And I can assure you, this hurts your respect, image, and chances of being promoted in the organization. Such encounters also leave you open to the possibility of sexual harassment, perhaps the most dangerous threat of them all. This is yet another example of exercising self-restraint, and keeping true focus on your priority—your career.

Also be very cautious of entering into a dating relationship with a client or vendor. These can be especially delicate in regard to your company's image and position with another company. You could be compromising that position and jeopardizing your career, as you are a professional representative of your company. Don't blow it.

In most cases, these examples are issues of judgment, not necessarily breaking company policy. According to an American Management Association (AMA) survey released in February 2003, *"84 percent of respondents said that their companies had no written policies on workplace or employee dating, compared to 12 percent of companies that had policies; four percent of respondents did not know whether such a policy existed. Of the companies where policies did exist, 11 percent prohibit any co-worker from dating, whereas the majority of companies prohibit employees from dating a subordinate (92%) or a superior (69%)."*

In a 2004 feature article on *Monster.com* titled "Danger: Office Romance Ahead...Five Reasons Not to Date Your Coworker," author Roberta Chinsky Matuson concluded, *"So before you pencil in a date with your office desire, schedule dinner with some nonwork-related friends. You'd be surprised what might happen if you start nurturing your other relationships. If you spend a little more time away from the office and your coworkers, you might just give Cupid a chance to improve his aim."*

Recommended Books

Office Romance: Playing with Fire without Getting Burned
Dennis M. Powers – Amacom, 1998

Sex at Work: Attraction, Orientation, Harassment, Flirtation and Discrimination
Mari Florence, Ed Fortson – Silver Lake Publishing, 2000

Don't Let Sexual Harassment Ruin Your Career Before It Begins

Most companies should have a sexual harassment prevention program that will include a manual, video, or employee orientation. Pay attention. I guarantee you will learn at least one thing about what is appropriate and what is not. And knowing this difference could save your career down the road.

> **?** *Is it a violation to tell jokes using provocative language?*
>
> **?** *Is it a violation to ask an employee out for a date if he/she is in a lower level position than you are?*
>
> **?** *Is it a violation to leave romantic notes and candy for someone as a secret admirer?*

If you don't know these answers, you need to. For better or worse, these things happen every day in the office environment. Often policies vary from company to company, and laws vary from state to state. You could be fired, heavily fined, or kept from earning raises or promotions, even if your intent wasn't malicious or harassing. Try explaining that reason for discharge at your next interview.

> *Common examples of sexual harassment include:*
>
> ☒ "Quid pro quo," or "something for something," where someone offers a professional favor in exchange for a date, or sexual favors.
>
> ☒ Unnecessary physical contact, such as a "pat on the butt," a "tickle of the ribs," or a neck rub.
>
> ☒ Displaying a graphic item within the workplace, such as a nude or offensive swimsuit calendar.
>
> ☒ Discussing details, facts, or rumors of someone's private intimate matters.
>
> ☒ Staring, "checking someone out," or the use of "elevator eyes," such as scanning someone from head-to-toe as they walk by.

Most people are aware when staring or elevator eyes are aimed at them. In a singles bar, the level of acceptance might be much different. But in the professional environment, it can make people feel very uncomfortable, pressured, and distraught.

Getting involved in certain sticky situations may not necessarily be illegal, but may be examples of very poor professional judgment. Know what is right and wrong, and do what is right. There is too much at stake in your career. Such situations can affect your image, reputation, and respect within the company.

Approximately 15,000 sexual harassment cases are submitted each year to the Equal Employment Opportunity Commission (EEOC). And, yes ladies, sexual harassment does go both ways. According to the EEOC, 11% of those cases involve men filing against female supervisors.

If you ever feel you are a victim of sexual harassment, you should step forward immediately, and follow company procedures. Your human resources department should be trained to document the situation and take the appropriate steps necessary to investigate the charges and begin potential action. There are also many legal safeguards that protect you if you fear retaliation for stepping forward.

Recommended Books

Unwelcome and Unlawful:
Sexual Harassment in the American Workplace
Raymond F. Gregory – Cornell University Press, 2004

Step Forward: Sexual Harassment in the Workplace:
What You Need to Know!
Susan L. Webb – Master Media Pub Corp, 1997

Recommended Websites

www.lawguru.com/faq/16.html
www.legal-database.com/laborlaw.htm
www.workforce.com
www.washrag.org

Chapter Seven:

Spectacular Career Development

Strive To Be The Best At What You Do

OK, so now you know what to do and what not to do in an every-day office environment. Now, let's take your career to the next level. Spectacular career development doesn't begin with clever tips or tricks you can use to schmooze your boss. It begins with being extremely dedicated to perform your job to the best of your ability. Be truly great at what you do every day, and take pride in your work throughout your career. In the end, the cream does rise to the top.

Most people have some type of professional aspiration, whether they are aware of it or not. It may be greater income, greater responsibility, job security, or perhaps it is even lifestyle-related. Whatever your motivation, it takes perseverance, focus, and self-discipline to achieve your goals. As mentioned before, there is no substitute for hard work. You must be prepared to earn your success in life.

"Focus on striving and thriving, not just surviving."

Staying focused means devoting your full mental and physical energies toward your objective. Staying focused in your career during your 20's will be a tremendous challenge. In this incredible world in which we live, it is very easy to become distracted. Certainly, within your position, there will be plenty of tasks and job responsibilities to juggle every day. To many, that will be a new challenge in itself.

But, as discussed, there are also many other outside personal diversions, such as friends, family, hobbies, entertainment, bills, and other responsibilities. While important, time invested with all of these items can be considered counter-productive to achieving your professional goals. You have to determine what you must do to succeed, and what you must sacrifice. Just as with dieting, conquering an addiction, or training for a marathon, self-discipline is the key to success. It also requires self-discipline to manage your activities in regard to your priorities.

"If something is important enough to you, you'll make time for it."

Michael Jordan was the first one in the gym to practice throughout his career, even though everyone else needed to practice more than he. Super Bowl XXXV MVP Ray Lewis stayed home and studied extra film of upcoming opponents, while his teammates hit the town every night. Do you want to achieve like a champion, or do you want to be just like everyone else?

The work environment is a unique one. It is one that combines teamwork and competition within that team framework at the same time. This is similar to athletics, where two players at the same position both compete for the starting job. Within a company, competing for a promotion, award, or even to simply be "#1 in performance" should be considered friendly competition. However, there can often be a lot at stake.

So, how will your performance stack up against others? Constantly try to improve your skills, and be willing to outwork the competition. Focus on quality with every project or task. Take performance reviews to heart, and consider it a challenge to develop in the areas your manager identifies. View each of these areas not as problems, but as opportunities. Always strive to be the best at what you do.

Besides the pride of becoming the best at what you do, there are strategic career advantages. Companies want to find and hire the best, and they are willing to pay much more for them. You want to become talented enough, produce good enough results, and eventually acquire enough experience performing *"X"* that you are in demand. This may be in a position or industry where it is difficult to find a qualified person who knows how to do *"X."* Or, you may be able to become the main source of expertise and resource on *"X,"* so that people might seem helpless without you. This will also help you gain the ultimate job security. When there is a demand for what you do, you can command a higher salary. If you do something that everyone knows how to do, or everyone else can do just as well as you, you can't command anything—you get what you get.

Perpetual Self-Promotion

> *"If a tree falls in the forest, but no one hears it,*
> *does it make a sound?"*

> *"If you do something great, but no one knows about it,*
> *is it really great?"*

Once you have established yourself as great at what you do, you must find ways to let people know about it. During the graduate marketing program at Webster University in St. Louis, I completed Marketing 5500, titled *Professional Seminars in Marketing: Promoting Yourself.* It involved creating a strategic marketing plan toward promoting your career. What a tremendous exercise (and to think my company provided tuition reimbursement for that class)!

Promotion involves making your target audience aware of your product. Your target market may include professionals both within your company and outside your company. Everyone is their own product, and everyone is their own strategic planner and publicity agent. No one else will do this for you, so you have to. But, that's OK. This can often be a fun task. Everyone enjoys bragging about themselves, right?

If that seems a bit uncomfortable, consider what a resume is. People certainly don't submit an additional page with their resume that outlines *"reasons not to hire me"* to be objective. And trust me, the other people who earn awards and promotions are bragging, too. Perpetual self-promotion isn't optional, it's essential.

Start accumulating items in a portfolio. This portfolio may include awards, articles you wrote, articles you were quoted in, certifications you've earned, letters of praise, etc. Keep these items clean and organized, and bring them to any future interviews you have throughout your career. You should always continue to build on your portfolio.

Submit your promotions, awards, or other successes in university and alumni organization updates. You never know who might be reading it. Another alum might be looking to replace a position in your field, and you could get contacted out of the blue. Submit your own press releases to local newspapers or community magazines:

"Local Businesswoman Wins AMA Award"

Sometimes, there is just no substitute for someone seeing your name in print. Volunteer to write an article in the company newsletter, or better yet, in a trade magazine. Many editors are starving for articles and material. Submit the article along with your credentials, and—shazam—*you've been published!* A printed article will look good in your portfolio and look impressive on your resume.

With your college education, company experience, membership in a professional organization, and authorship, you are now well on your way to separating yourself from others, and creating demand for "your product." At some point, you can certainly pursue writing a book in your field, as well. The rest of your life, you can always be known as the *"Author of…XYZ."* Your efforts may even lead to fame or national recognition within your field.

Further, you could pursue teaching the subject of your expertise at a local college. Often, colleges are looking for last-minute replacement instructors for evening or summer school. Not only can you add to your resume that you "taught this subject at the University of . . . ," but you can get paid while doing it.

Self-promotion also includes your networking skills, which will be covered in more detail later this chapter. How you and your achievements are perceived by everyone you come in contact with may be the most powerful promotional tool you have. However, be careful not to come across as bragging too much. There are modest ways to communicate your talents and accomplishments to people.

It may be sad to say, but self-promotion is one of the biggest keys to your career success. Always strive to keep an entrepreneurial attitude in this area. Never stop thinking about this—it is ongoing until the day you retire. Similar to office politics, there are other factors present besides performance that determine success. Image and perception are two of those factors.

"Image is everything."

What exactly is the image you want to project? Is it that of a star? Then you must do the things that stars do. You may just want to be considered experienced, knowledgeable, nice, or a true team player. Each day, you need to be thinking of what you need to do to enhance that image. Image is work, it doesn't just happen. Everyone has an image, whether they like it or not. Figure out what you want yours to be, then make it happen.

Recommended Books

The Brand You50 (Reinventing Work):
Fifty Ways to Transform Yourself from an Employee into
a Brand That Shouts Distinction, Commitment, and Passion!
Tom Peters – Knopf Publishing Group, 1999

Promoting Yourself: 52 Lessons for Getting to the Top . . .
and Staying There
Hal Lancaster – Free Press, 2004

Creating You & Co: Learn to Think Like the CEO of Your Own Career
William Bridges – Perseus Publishing, 1998

50 Ways To Get Promoted, Nathan G. Jensen – Bookworld Services, 1999

How to Shine at Work, Linda Dominguez – McGraw-Hill, 2003

How to Publish Your Articles: A Complete Guide to Making
the Right Publication Say Yes
Shirley Kawa-Jump – Square One Publishers, 2001

If Your First Job Is Indeed Not The Right One For You...

"The grass is always greener on the other side"

This philosophy is followed by disgruntled employees every day. Yet, in reality, this simply gives false hope to many who think escaping a terrible job, terrible boss, or terrible clients will solve all of their problems. Then they discover their same problems follow them wherever they go, because *they* are the common denominator. If you continue to believe in that philosophy, and you keep leaving jobs, you will have completed a full circle by the end of your career—ending at the same level you began.

Consider getting another job as a last resort. One important principle here: Do not become what hiring managers call a "jumper." If you are going to make a move, be sure it is the right move for you. Don't just "give it another shot somewhere else." It is very important to show consistency and stability within one position, or one company, on your resume.

You do not want to have a resume that has four different companies listed within the last 18 months, or even four years. I once had a client who wanted me to give a final interview to an individual the hiring managers liked. He sounded good. Yet, I raised the concern that he had four positions since college graduation, and had not proven sustained success at any one of those positions. So, why would we think this position would be any different? This individual was not hired.

"Why do we want to spend our money to recruit, hire, train, and develop someone who will leave within 6 months or a year?"

Think about it—hiring someone is an investment to a company. Since 1990, companies are increasingly realizing the costs associated with the entire process of recruiting, hiring, training, and developing. High employee turnover is quite damaging to a company. It hurts profitability, operational flow, customer service, morale, etc. Companies need serious career professionals they can invest their resources in and depend on for many years. If you are considered a "jumper," you will find it much more difficult to get hired. If you do have several positions within a short period of time listed on your resume, be sure you are prepared to clearly explain the reason for leaving each position.

Remember, you will be starting from scratch with a new company. You have to make all new impressions, and you will be on the bottom of the seniority scale once again. Therefore, make sure a job change is the right move for you. Go through the checklist of what your current job truly offers you, and what the real reason for your departure is.

> **?** *Do you like what you are doing?*
>
> **?** *Is there an opportunity for advancement if you stay?*
>
> **?** *Do you like going to work? If not, are the barriers to your unhappiness correctable or will they be there forever?*
>
> **?** *Do you like your boss?*
>
> **?** *Do you like your co-workers?*
>
> **?** *Is this job developing you for the next step in your career?*
>
> **?** *Are you leaving just because of one person?*
>
> **?** *Is the company and/or industry headed in the right direction?*

If you have determined that this job is indeed not the right one for you, be strategic. Don't be unemployed. Pursue your next opportunity while you are still employed. First, it shows stability. Second, you won't go without a paycheck. Third, it is easier to get a job when already you have a job. If you are jobless, you now seem desperate, and you have less value to employers. You are bargaining from a position of weakness rather than a position of strength. This is a principle you will always need to know, even 20 years down the road.

Never leave a job as part of a knee-jerk reaction. Never get frustrated or fed up, and blurt out a spontaneous *"I quit."* Try explaining that on your next interview: *"I just got mad and quit that day. So, now I am looking for a new job."*

No matter how bad it gets, take a deep breath, get through the day, go home, and begin logically planning your next career move. Always try finding another position first, and always provide at least two weeks notice. When you do leave a company or organization, there are two ways to do it: the professional way or the unprofessional way. Be a professional. Never burn bridges. Always wish everyone in the company the best of luck *(whether you mean it or not).*

Discreetly go through your computer files and cabinet files for anything that may be of resource to you later. Take them home with you the night before you notify your employer of your resignation—just in case they tell you to leave right then and there. Be careful not to take confidential or proprietary information of the company. Don't underestimate what items may be helpful to you even 5 or 10 years down the road. Heck, I referred to several items from my first job in writing this book!

It is very unfortunate to say, but quite often the best way to receive raises in this world is to switch companies. Loyalty between the employee and the company is not what it should be, on either end. Most companies think backwards when trying to retain their most valued, talented employees. Sometimes companies are willing to pay more, or offer "signing bonuses," to external candidates that they won't offer to internal candidates for the same position. There are caps on internal raises and pay scales are rigid.

Thus, you can often have a better chance at a quick jump in salary by leaving. For instance, a typical annual raise for most company employees ranges from 2%-6%. This is compared to the chance of a 10%-50% increase if you land a better position at another company. This is a shame, because the original company paid to recruit, train, and develop you—and now the other company will benefit from that training and development.

In certain, but rare situations, your company may try to "match" the competitive salary offer to keep you. But don't ever start with that in mind, and believe you can simply use that as a negotiating tool for a raise. More than likely, you are more expendable than you believe. Besides, this could create some hard feelings within your company if you decide to stay. This is not the best strategy to get yourself a raise.

Often, many skills are easily transferable into different markets or fields. This is important, because your area of expertise may be impacted by consumer trends or technological changes along the way. You need to see those changes before they happen and adapt accordingly. Unfortunately, many people get blind-sided after being in the same industry or company for 20 years, then suddenly become a victim of downsizing. They may have had a false sense of security, and didn't really believe things would change, so they did not have the foresight to prepare. Be on the cutting edge of technology and keep up with current events within your field—always—throughout your career.

If you are unhappy, not performing well, or feel out of place in your job, perhaps you are simply not cut out for that industry. Your talents may be better suited in a different field or type of position. If you see repetitive failure or challenges you can't seem to overcome, you might want to consider this. Everyone has their "calling." Just try not to go too far in life before you discover what your "calling" is.

It's OK to switch careers. Don't panic. You may feel that many of your previous efforts have gone to waste. However, if you sense an opportunity that is right for you and will lead to better success and greater happiness, go for it. You are still young.

I have had several people borrow my job search files because word got out that I had resume resources, a list of HR contacts, job search websites, interview tips worksheets, etc. I was the person people came to when they wanted a career switch. Back then, I was a free career coach!

Always keep your job search resources on file. You never know when another career search may start again. It may start on your own initiative, or you may become a sudden victim of downsizing. Perhaps you had an interview somewhere and you either didn't get the offer, or you didn't accept it. Don't throw anything away. You can never have too many hiring managers and HR managers as contacts, and you can never have too many companies in which you have at least one contact. These resources will also serve as a great refresher for what needs to be done in a job search.

Lastly, always keep your updated resume on file. You never know when you'll run into that one terrific break from someone who says *"send me over your resume tomorrow and let's see what we can do."* Always keep your eyes open and be ready to seize a great opportunity.

Recommended Books

I Don't Know What I Want, but I Know It's Not This:
A Step-By-Step Guide to Finding Gratifying Work
Julie Jansen – Penguin Books, 2003

Change Your Job, Change Your Life: Careering and Re-Careering
in the New Boom/Bust Economy
Ronald L. Krannich – Impact Publications, 2002

Fire Your Boss
Stephen M. Pollan, Mark Levine – Harper Resource, 2004

Networking 101: Make Contacts, Keep In Contact With Your Contacts, And Never Burn Bridges

It will amaze you throughout your professional career how small of a world we actually live in. You can never know enough people or have too many contacts. It is estimated that everyone you know knows 250 people, and those 250 people also know 250 people, and so on. Mathematically, that is a powerful network of potential contacts!

Imagine a time two, five, or ten years from now where you need a new job. If you have enough contacts that know you and your reputation, you will save yourself time and effort sending out resumes to strangers. And, you will more than likely find a much better opportunity.

"It's not what you know, but who you know."

I got my first job out of college through networking. My fraternity brother's girlfriend (now wife) got me an interview at her company. I landed a job with my second company through the low-percentage chance of responding to an ad in the local newspaper. Though I didn't gain the opportunity through networking, I was able to name-drop during my interview with the president about a common individual we both knew professionally. Three years later, I was recruited by an old college friend to become the sales manager at another company.

Professionals that know a lot of people find a way to go further in their career. But keep in mind, you still need to be as polished as possible regarding resume development and interviewing skills. Networking can only get you so far. If you are a clown, you won't get the job.

There are countless benefits to networking that go well beyond getting your next job. There will be countless examples of you or your company needing assistance from someone. Suppose you have a problem installing new software on your PC, or you need advice on a legal matter.

"I know someone who does that!"

Not that this is the intent, but having connections has plenty of perks. I got free tickets to numerous sporting events, concerts, and other select functions. I got discounts on clothes, furniture, and automobiles because I knew employees at those stores. I found my accountant, my financial advisor, and even the person who cuts my hair through contacts I had with other people.

"If I could have done one thing different over the past 10 years...

...I would have kept track of every person I came in contact with since college."

Generally speaking, I am an organized people-person with a good memory. I also believe I have done an above-average job of keeping up with people during the past 10 years. With that being said, there are so many other people that I've lost contact with, it's truly depressing. Some may have been people whose names I now can't even remember.

Professionally speaking, there are a countless number of times I could have used someone's help. From a personal standpoint, I have met so many people whom I found interesting or simply enjoyed their company. Yet today, I wouldn't even know how to contact them. I would just like to hear from them and see how they are doing. Time and people pass by so fast in life.

"Yeah, whatever happened to Kevin Crawford anyway? I always liked him."

Therefore, my major piece of advice is this: Keep everyone you know on file, using Microsoft Outlook®, Microsoft Access®, Microsoft Excel®, or sales software such as "ACT!®" Keep their name, address, phone number, e-mail address, company, and title saved. Also include a field for additional comments, such as children or hobbies. Collect business cards from people and enter them into your master file as you go. Try your best to keep in touch with people from day one after college. Make phone calls every three to six months to people you'd like to stay in contact with, and update your files periodically. At a minimum, send out holiday cards at the end of each year.

"Keep making new contacts, and stay in contact with those contacts."

If you don't stay in contact with your contacts, you might as well forget ever asking them for anything. If you have a job interview with a company your contact works for, you will feel a little foolish calling them after 5 years and saying:

You: *"It's good to talk to you again. How are the wife and kids? By the way, I need your help."*

Contact: *"If you cared so much about me, why haven't you called me in five years?"*

One friend of mine was a manager at a major electronics store. He got a call from one of our college buddies that he had not heard from in over six years. Within 30 seconds, he asked *"Can you get me a discount on a refrigerator?"* That's not networking, that's audacity.

It's important to get the right kind of contacts, as well. Consider the group of people you "hang out with." Are they a positive influence on you? Hopefully, yes. Try to surround yourself and associate with positive, ambitious, and successful people throughout your career. Learn from them, and they will help you raise the bar for yourself. These people usually know more of the right kind of contacts, as well.

Keep in contact with your favorite professors or university administrators. They love to hear about the lives of former students. They can provide advice, contacts, or even letters of recommendation well into your career.

It is amazing how many connections you will get from extra-curricular activities. Play in a softball league, take a cooking class, get involved in the neighborhood, anything. Again, your career advancement depends more on the people you interact with during your career than the knowledge you've gained from all the books you've ever read *(except this one)*. Always be sure to return favors, and take extra time and effort to help others when they may need your help professionally. Remember, what goes around comes around. Thus, never burn bridges. *Repeating:* NEVER burn bridges. And, lastly, don't forget to be nice to people. Having a lot of contacts won't do you much good if none of them like you.

Recommended Books

How to Create Your Own Luck: The "You Never Know" Approach to Networking, Taking Chances, and Opening Yourself to Opportunity
Susan RoAne – Wiley Business Trade Books, 2004

Referral of a Lifetime, Tim Templeton – Berrett-Koehler, 2004

Masters of Networking
Ivan R. Misner, Don Morgan – Bard Press (TX), 2000

Recommended Websites

www.rileyguide.com/support.html
www.itsnotwhatyouknow.com
www.ryze.com
www.network.monster.com

Get Involved! Join Professional And Alumni Organizations

This piece of advice has been mentioned briefly in previous chapters. Join professional and alumni organizations. It's easy. There are only over *100,000* to choose from. Make a commitment to join at least two. You will learn, develop—and yes—network!

The *Encyclopedia of Associations* provides a listing of all active organizations, but there may be additional local or informal groups in your area that may be of benefit to you. Consider joining local networking groups, *especially* if you are in sales. Ask your mentor what organizations are worthwhile and relevant to your industry. More than likely, they are already a member. Some examples include:

☑ Chamber of Commerce	☑ Neighborhood
☑ Church	☑ Alumni
☑ Professional	☑ Volunteer
☑ Philanthropic	☑ Hobby
☑ Athletic	☑ Online Communities

You may think everyone joins such groups, but the fact is most people don't. Most young employees get off work and go to happy hours with their friends or go home and watch television. Joining organizations shows others that you are serious about your career and serious about learning more within your profession. Again, it is OK to have recreation time, just remember to balance it with your professional priorities, as well.

When attending periodic events, be sure to trade plenty of business cards and take an interest in other people. Don't spend too long with one person—move about and mingle. And don't stand by the free appetizers all night and be a "grazer." Nobody likes a "grazer."

As you become more seasoned and successful, turn around and be available for others, and become a mentor when you have the opportunity. It is rewarding. You may find you enjoy it so much, you will want to teach or train in your field someday. Stay involved and give back to your community, college, organizations, and people who helped you become successful. Most alumni associations charge only a modest annual fee for joining, and typically provide benefits such as a helpful website, newsletter, access to contacts, and news related to your field.

Now, there are critics who believe many of these organizations could be a waste of time and money. Given which chapter you consider, that could be the case. But, at least do your homework to find out for yourself.

☺ *You may land that one key connection from networking.*

☺ *You could learn professional content that helps you in your job.*

☺ *You just may meet new friends who are in the same point in their career as you.*

More often than not, I am a supporter of getting involved. What else are you doing to promote your career that 2nd Tuesday night of every month? You don't have to join every one, but find the organizations most beneficial to you – and really get involved. The more you put into something, the more you will get out of it.

Continuing Education: Grad School Or No Grad School?

Many students enter graduate school directly after undergraduate school as a full-time student. If you have the ability to take advantage of that opportunity, that is terrific. Most others have to pursue a graduate degree while they are working a full-time job during the day. Obtaining your masters degree or Ph.D. at night takes dedication, discipline, and long hours of work. It may also take more money, or more student loans.

However, many companies now offer tuition reimbursement programs to their employees. This is one benefit you need to consider when deciding where to work in the first place, if you believe graduate school may be in your future. This can save students thousands of dollars. If tuition reimbursement is offered at your company, this is an open invitation for you to at least consider the opportunity. Be careful, as many companies who offer this require you to stay within the company for a period of time thereafter, or they will pursue repayment from you later.

Everyone should at least *consider* graduate school. What does *consider* mean? It means research the facts, and identify the pros and cons of the decision. Is the investment of your time, effort, and money worth it to your career? Depending on the field, it may or may not be. Consult your college career center or seek resources on the Internet to determine if post-graduate degrees actually lead to greater income or opportunity within your profession.

Seek out those with a masters or doctorate in your field of interest. Ask them about the program they went through and if it was beneficial to their career. You may get varying answers. Get input from HR managers and vice presidents of divisions and companies you want to work for. Ask them how important earning a post-graduate degree is when they decide to hire and promote. You will get entirely different responses based on your industry and the degree. This is critical!

Generally speaking, the median annual income is just over $12,000 higher for those posessing a masters degree, as opposed to those posessing a bachelor's degree, according to the 2000 census. Further, obtaining a masters degree can give candidates a better chance of getting a job in the first place vs. undergraduate competition, especially in a tough job market.

Aside from the financial advantages of a graduate degree, there is a certain amount of respect, prestige, and credibility that you will garner the rest of your career. The experience can also be intellectually stimulating *(if that appeals to you)*, and you will interact with many higher-level contacts in your area of expertise.

Understand that a masters degree or Ph.D. is something that "no one can ever take away from you." Even if you may not see a direct benefit in your immediate future, it could give you an edge with a different company and a different position *20 years from now.* If you do earn a graduate degree while working during the day, you have an advantage over those who went straight to graduate school from undergraduate school as a full-time student. They are graduating with a masters degree. You are graduating with a masters degree and career experience.

If you think graduate school is for you, my advice is *don't wait around!* Arrange to take graduate entrance exams, such as the GRE (Graduate Record Examination) or GMAT (Graduate Management Admissions Test), while the knowledge is still fresh in your mind. Research graduate schools and degree options right away, then go for it. I have heard this advice from many other professionals who waited 10, 20, or even 30 years after graduating to begin their graduate work. It is much tougher to re-enter the academic environment after you have been removed for so long. You may have a spouse, children, much greater responsibilities at work, or the requirement of travel in your job.

It is also difficult to get back those disciplined study habits you gained during undergraduate school *(right?)*. Besides, do you want your degree sooner or later? Would you choose between earning it at age 25 or 35? If you earn it at 25, you can then benefit from that degree during those next 10 years, helping accelerate your career path even more. So, if it is indeed right for you, why wait? Go get it!

Recommended Books

Graduate Schools in the US 2004
Peterson's Guides, 2003

The College Board Index of Majors & Graduate Degrees 2004
College Board, 2003

Dan Cassidy's Worldwide Graduate Scholarship Directory
Dan Cassidy – Career Press, 2000

Cash for Grad School
Phillip C. McKee, Cynthia Ruiz McKee
Harper Resource, 2004

Getting Money For Graduate School
Peterson's Guides, 2002

The Graduate School Funding Handbook
April Vahle Hamel, Mary Morris Heiberger, Julia Miller Vick
University of Pennsylvania Press, 2002

Recommended Websites

www.gradview.com
www.graduateguide.com
www.gradschools.com
www.petersons.com
www.mba.com/mba
www.wiredscholar.com/paying
http://scholarships.brokescholar.com/

Chapter Eight:

Planning Your Ultimate Road to Success

Leadership And The Management Ladder

"Be a leader, not a follower."

Some companies hire college graduates directly into management or supervisory roles. Most do not. Most hire into entry-level positions, which offer an opportunity to manage only after one has excelled in the entry-level position. One reason for this is because employees need to "pay their dues" and gain experience. But another is that these companies don't believe young professionals are *prepared*, or have the skills to be a leader or manager yet.

Companies are dying for good managers and future leaders. They are hard to find. Methods for recruiting and developing leaders have become more organized and progressive in recent years. There is a system in most major companies for "succession planning," in which the company attempts to identify and groom candidates who would be ready to step into higher positions if called upon, even immediately if needed.

Put Yourself on a Fast Developmental Track

As an employee, you will have a classified employee file. In this file, companies may categorize you as "high potential," "average," "low potential," etc. Once you are labeled as "high potential," the organization will find ways to push you along throughout your career. There are also categories saved in a corporate database listing your preparation level for promotion. You might be listed as *"Ready Now"* or *"Ready in Two Years"* based on your performance, development, and potential.

Find out how you can be put on a career fast track and be labeled as one of these future leaders. What are the keys to achieving this? First, you must make an impression on your boss. You must also meet and impress members of upper management. Further, you must meet and impress organizational development or human resources specialists, who facilitate such succession and development programs. These people will assist you in creating a career development outline and consider what other departments may fit you well in the future. These plans are aligned with what your skill set is and what your ultimate career goals are.

More companies are offering such formalized programs for employee development today. I participated in such a program at my first company called the "Emerging Leader Series." Often, these programs aren't overly publicized. You may be invited upon hiring, recommended to participate by management, or you may have to seek the program out and be approved to enter.

Along with participating in such programs, you must prove your dedication in other ways to truly be on the *"fast track."* You may have to be willing to take on extra assignments, be available to relocate, and undergo additional training or education. Being willing to relocate doesn't just allow for more opportunities; it also shows that you are dedicated to the company. This will help put you in a top-tier bracket, ready to be promoted at an opening anywhere at any time.

Is Management or Leadership Your Goal?

Some people will seek out leadership positions in the working world, as that is their goal. Others may not. Yet, almost everyone will be placed in situations during their career that require them to take action, make a tough decision, or be responsible for impacting others.

If you are one who plans on simply finding a job you love, and doing that job every day, that's fine. However, you may find that you will enjoy teaching or sharing the skills and knowledge you have with others. That could just mean serving as an informal leader of a department. Or, this may open the possibility of you wanting to become a manager, or even a trainer in your area of expertise some day.

Some people believe leaders are born. However, many individual leadership skills can be developed over time. Everyone should pursue management and leadership development opportunities, especially if this may already be a gap or weakness for them. There are many such resources in the professional world today, which include a multitude of books, tapes, seminars, and corporate training programs. Participation will help young professionals grow, whether they strive to be the next CEO or simply improve their own management skills.

Challenges of a Young Manager

There are several problematic scenarios that involve the inexperienced or first-time manager in business today. Often, young managers try too hard to be liked and accepted among those they are managing. But unfortunately, tough decisions may not always be popular. Also, young managers frequently try to do everything themselves, take things too personally, and take all the blame. This leads to unhappiness and burnout.

The other extreme is when young managers use their position as an opportunity to exert power for the sake of exerting power, and boosting their ego. This may lead to resentment and dislike from employees. You have to earn the respect of employees who are older and who have been with the company longer. It won't just be given or assumed. This is a difficult challenge to overcome.

Another problem involves employees who get promoted because they are so good at doing their job that upper management decided to make them a manager. The problem is, a good worker does not automatically equal a good manager. This happens quite frequently in technology, production, customer service, and sales environments. Those promoted may not possess the social skills or leadership skills to succeed in such an entirely different role. They often believe *"I did it this way, so this is the only way it should be done."*

Being a Good Manager Is Difficult

Management can take a lot of hard work, and can lead to a lot of headaches. To be a good manager, you have to do the little things and focus on them every day. You will be challenged to motivate people, discipline people, and direct people. You will have to address morale issues, performance issues, and all other personnel issues with your employees. You may have to build and develop your own team. This requires recruiting, interviewing, and hiring skills. You must then be sure your employees are in a position to succeed.

☑ Are they clear about their job responsibilities?

☑ Are they properly trained?

☑ Do they have the resources necessary to succeed?

☑ Are they motivated and inspired?

☑ Is there a system in place to track performance and provide feedback?

☑ Has a performance improvement and personal development plan been created for the employee?

The result of your work determines the result of their work. Ultimately, you are responsible for your own performance, and all of theirs. The better your employees perform, the better you look. And, you always want to look good. Thus, your management skills may be the most important skills you will ever have.

Talk to your mentor about what their feelings are on management. Also, try to remember all of the managers you have had in your life, even if it was at a fast-food restaurant. What did they do that you liked? What did they do that made you work harder? What did they do that de-motivated you? I believe I have taken at least one thing from every boss I have ever had—even the ones I didn't like.

Every college and university should require its students to take at least one course in management before they graduate, no matter what the major. Chances are very high that between the ages of 22-60, you will have at least one employee reporting to you at some point during your career. The problem is that curriculums are so focused on specific content that general management skills are often overlooked. College graduates are trained to "do something" or "know something" in a specific field, but their management skills are lacking. This is why management seminars are so popular in the corporate world. Know your trade, but also learn how to become a good leader and a good manager.

Recommended Books

The New Supervisor: How to Thrive in Your First Year As a Manager
Martin M. Broadwell, Carol Broadwell Dietrich
Perseus Books Group, 1998

The First Time Manager
Loren Belker – Amacom, 1997

Management Skills for New Managers
Carol Ellis – Amacom, 2004

The Accidental Manager: Get the Skills You Need to Excel in Your New Career
Gary S. Topchik – Amacom, 2003

Leadership Passages: The Personal and Professional Transitions That Make or Break a Leader
David Dotlich, James L. Noel, Norman Walker
Wiley Business Trade Books, 2004

Recommended Seminars

"Management Skills for First-Time Supervisors"
National Seminars Group, www.natsem.com, 1-800-258-7246

"Essential Skills for First-Time Managers or Supervisors"
Fred Pryor Seminars, www.careertrack.com, 1-800-556-3009

"Excelling as a First-Time Manager or Supervisor"
Skillpath Seminars, www.skillpath.com, 1-800-873-7545

Is A Job In Sales Right For You? Consider These Points...

When I was in college, I had a warped vision of people in sales. I always pictured a shoe salesperson at the mall or a door-to-door vacuum cleaner salesperson. Then I heard horror stories of friends who went into full-commission sales positions right after college. They bounced from job-to-job selling copiers, long-distance services, computer supplies—they seemed miserable. I thought sales was so low on the company totem pole, I wouldn't ever consider it. Boy, was I wrong!

My mentor at my first company was the first one to open my eyes. He said, *"The salespeople are gods here. They say jump, and 3,000 people at headquarters ask 'how high?'"* Then it started to dawn on me; he was right. Every company in this country is bankrupt without sales. And if sales doesn't sell, you don't have a job. It's the most important position in the company.

But sales is tough. Waiting until the end of the month hoping you've sold enough to pay your rent is pressure—especially if you have a family depending on it. You must be prepared to face constant rejection for the rest of your career. This occupation is proven to lead to a higher risk of alcoholism, divorce, suicide, and heart attack. Sounds enticing, doesn't it?

So, why do people go into sales? The adrenaline rush ignited from closing a huge deal is unlike any other that can be gained from a salaried position. And let's face it, there is pressure with every job. Every employee is paid to perform some function, reaching certain required standards, in a certain amount of time. There are not too many jobs in this world without some degree of pressure.

There can also be great benefits if you are successful. Salespeople are in charge of how much they make, not the company. What a profession—*"Who wants to pick your own salary? Come on down!"* No matter how well $30,000 employees do their job over the course of a year, they will still be paid $30,000. Salespeople could have a great year and quadruple their income over the previous year. And the prizes, perks, and awards will come rolling in as well. It has been said that if you can sell, you can write your ticket anywhere. There will always be someone wanting to hire you, and offer you an even better compensation plan if you're worth it.

But be careful, as there are bad sales jobs and fantastic sales jobs. There are many industries in which salespeople are paid particularly high incomes. They include medical, chemical, financial, computer/technical, and business-to-business products and services. The more expertise required, the more income the position demands. Thus, no matter what your field, you should at least consider this avenue at some point if you also have personal and presentation skills to add. This can be a very lucrative combination.

I truly believe the greatest oversight in our college curriculum today is the absence of teaching the skill of sales. Millions of college students will have either a direct or indirect sales position at some point during their professional career. Besides, in the business world, it has been said that you sell yourself every day, which is true.

Yet there are very few college courses on sales. *(Marketing is related, but that doesn't count.)* This is one reason why the sales training field is so vast. There is a skill set required in sales like no other. There are many young professionals with industry knowledge, energy, and social skills, but who do not know how to sell.

There are a tremendous amount of powerful resources available in the field of sales. People are starving to learn how to succeed once they enter this field, and they never stop learning. Below is a list of resources on whether a position in sales is right for you, and, if so, how to start your successful sales career. Results of career assessments can be a good tool for determining this fit, as well.

OK, so you are not the suave, life-of-the-party personality that you think will succeed in sales? You'd be surprised how many successful salespeople I have met where I asked myself *"You mean to tell me YOU are the top salesperson?"* Hard work, product/industry knowledge, and networking skills are the keys to their success. So, don't be intimidated when considering this option either right away or down the road. You just might be good at it!

Recommended Books

Your First Year in Sales: Making the Transition from Total Novice to Successful Professional
Tim Connor – Prima Lifestyles, 2001

Sales Careers: The Ultimate Guide to Getting a High-Paying Sales Job
Louise M. Kursmark, Edward R. Newill – JIST Publishing, 2003

The Accidental Salesperson: How to Take Control of Your Sales Career and Earn the Respect and Income You Deserve
Chris Lytle – Amacom, 2003

Recommended Websites

www.salesladder.com
www.salesjobs.com
www.salestrainingcamp.com
www.careerconceptsusa.com
www.salestrax.com
www.salesandmarketing.com

Is Entrepreneurship Right For You? Perhaps Someday...

Entrepreneurship Is Easy!

That's right, it is easy to become an entrepreneur. In most states, you can head to the Secretary of State Office, pay a modest fee of typically $100 - $200, pick a name for your company, and you are officially an entrepreneur!

Now, more than likely, entrepreneurship is not for you...quite yet. It often takes a tremendous amount of knowledge, experience, capital, and resourcefulness to start your own company, and the odds are against you. It also encompasses all of the qualities of leadership, management, sales, self-promotion, and about everything else. Four out of five new businesses fail within the first year, and 98% of new businesses do not exist just 10 years later.

However, I would encourage you to consider it as an option throughout your career. On the optimistic side, 92% of U.S. business owners and 50% of millionaire entrepreneurs never even graduated from a 4-year college, according to Matthew Lesko in his book *"Free Money to Change Your Life."* Hard to believe, isn't it? Look at it this way—you are already one step ahead of them!

You can always consider starting a business "on the side" first during your full-time career. For instance, I know more than one person who has their own DJ company, where they work on nights and weekends after their day job. Other ideas include teaching, catering, web design, event planning, and—yes—wedding photography. This could be a good way to earn extra income or "test the waters" to determine if that could be a successful full-time endeavor for you. If you try this route, keep in mind—*you will be busy!* Remember, you will be the secretary, accountant, director of marketing, and CEO of your company. It can be overwhelming. However, did you know Microsoft, Hewlett-Packard, and Dell all began on part-time schedules, as well?

There are many advantages and disadvantages to consider with becoming an entrepreneur.

Advantages:
- ☺ Being your own boss
- ☺ Tax deductions
- ☺ Personally rewarding
- ☺ You keep the profits

Disadvantages:
- ☹ Risk
- ☹ Security
- ☹ No insurance/benefits
- ☹ Lots of hours

My suggestion is that you research and plan for your entrepreneurship thoroughly while you still have a job. This stage may take 30 days or 5 years, but the key is to be sure you have a plan first. If you have an idea, or are simply good at what you do, it's never too early to start brainstorming.

"Think outside of the box."

There are also the alternatives of operating a franchise or purchasing an existing company. Existing companies already have assets, employees, a presence in the market, and a client base. Be sure to consult someone who has experience with this first, and gather your resources regarding the use of business brokers, attorneys, banks, etc.

You must thoroughly research the financials, the operations, and the competition. You must also understand how you can make it more successful than the current ownership. If you're lucky, the business is running smoothly and profitably, and the owner is simply "ready to move on." However, these opportunities are tough to find—and the better the company is doing, the more expensive it is to purchase.

The Young Entrepreneurs Organization (YEO) is an outstanding resource and development group, and there are chapters throughout the United States. You do not have to actually own your own company to start getting involved and planning for such a time. There is no substitute for learning from people who have already done—and succeeded—at what you want to do. You will need help on where to turn for everything. The Small Business Administration (SBA) is available to you for loan possibilities and advice, as well as many other resources.

There are also a growing number of universities that now offer high-quality entrepreneurship degree programs, for both undergraduate and graduate students. *Entrepreneur* magazine ranked the Top 100 such programs in the May 2004 issue, which included the University of Arizona, Syracuse University, and Babson College near the top of the rankings.

Final suggestion on entrepreneurship: If you feel confident that you have the ability to survive and the opportunity to flourish, go for it! Although the odds are against you, you are more likely to attain the American dream of gaining great wealth in a short period of time by owning a business than by laboring 30 years climbing the corporate ladder. Even if you take a chance and fail, you can always try to re-enter the corporate world. So, keep your eyes open and consider viable opportunities that may present themselves. You may find this avenue quite rewarding.

Recommended Books

Generation Inc.: The 100 Best Businesses for Young Entrepreneurs
Elina Furman, Leah Furman – Penguin Putnam, 2000

Your First Business Plan
Joseph Covello, Brian Haselgren – SourceBooks 2002

Wealth Without a Job: The Entrepreneur's Guide to Freedom and Security Beyond the 9 to 5 Lifestyle
Phil Laut, Andy Fuehl – Wiley Business Trade Books, 2004

Buying and Selling a Business: A Step-by-Step Guide
Robert Klueger – Wiley Business Trade Books, 2004

The Unofficial Guide to Starting a Small Business
Marcia Layton Turner – Wiley Business Trade Books, 2004

The Complete Small Business Start-Up Guide
Lisa Rogak – Wiley Business Trade Books, 2004

Financing Your Small Business
James E. Burk, Richard P. Lehman – SourceBooks, 2004

Recommended Websites

www.sba.gov
www.yeo.org
www.score.org
www.franchising.org
www.sife.org
www.c-e-o.org

Where Is The Future Going, And Are You Going With It?

Many experts are optimistic about your generation, the "millennial generation," and the impact you will have on our society. Your generation tends to be positive, bright, technologically savvy, and possess a genuine concern about other people and the world. Your generation will develop new inventions, breakthrough cures, and advanced technologies in the future that we can only dream about today. You should be tremendously excited about this.

Life after college isn't just about the day after graduation. Your life after college will *(hopefully)* last a very long time. According to the U.S. National Center for Health Statistics, life expectancy is currently 77.2 years. This means that if you were born in 1984, you are projected to live until the year 2061. If you work until age 60, you will be working until the year 2044.

It is imperative to understand that the world we live in is constantly changing, and will change dramatically 5, 10, 20, and 40 years from now. But, what will change? And how will those changes impact your life and your career?

"The only constant in life is change."

The way that companies produce and sell their products and services is changing. The way consumers shop and purchase their products and services is also changing. There is continued growth in e-commerce, Internet downloads, online stock trading, real-time electronic transactions, and next-day delivery for seemingly everything.

In 2004, major PC manufacturer Gateway, Inc., decided to close all retail outlets and offer its products exclusively online. For it, inventory, retail employees, and "bricks-and-mortar" operations were too costly and inefficient to sustain. What will be next? By no means will shopping malls and retail stores cease to exist 20 years from now, but there are several products and services in which a direct-from-manufacturer sales and distribution process benefits both the company and consumer.

Trends such as the increased specialization of services and outsourcing will no doubt continue. There is continued development in automated man-ufacturing processes, robotics, and computer-run facilities. Advances with radio frequency identification (RFID) for products will provide immediate and extremely detailed information about everyday consumer behavior.

Such "smart-tags" will provide item-level tracking of individual products for manufacturers throughout the supply chain. Planning on shoplifting in the future? Similar RFID technology within those "smart tags" will follow you and that product home, where authorities will be waiting for you. Such capabilities are already installed on many recent-model vehicles on the road today.

We are entering a time of declining margins across many industries. Entities that were previously "cash cows" are now struggling. Some industries can be tremendously affected by the stock market, interest rates, political stability, and the economy in general. There are now more educated consumers with competitive information at their fingertips, and more global competition.

Without a doubt, we will continue to see the expansion of an increasing global market in the future. Experts see India and China continuing to grow as the two emerging economies of the next several decades. These markets are now offering tremendous opportunity to U.S. companies to sell their products and services, as well as efficiently outsourcing their production. Beyond traditional outsourcing, such as cheap manufacturing or unskilled labor to Mexico, these countries have provided a new wave of skilled cheap labor. This includes information technology services such as programming, web design, and even out-sourced accounting functions.

Other changes to consider about our future include:

 How will we be entertained in the future?

 How will our travel behaviors change in the future?

 How will our household products be different in the future?

 How will our methods of communication be different in the future?

 How will crime prevention, safety, and security be different in the future?

 How will our social and political environment affect business in the future?

 How will we train our employees and educate our students in the future?

You don't have to be responsible for changing the world. You can only try to be aware of how all of these changes will affect your industry, your company, and your career. For instance, teachers and trainers must have enhanced technical skills with the advent of computers in the classrooms, video-conferencing, online courses, and other e-learning methods.

But, how can you find out where the future is going? The vast majority of what you studied in college was from the past. What about the future? Of course, keep up with the news and current trends. There are some outstanding government-produced studies and projections available from the U.S. Bureau of Labor Statistics for almost every industry. Discover not only what industries are growing, but what companies, products, or trends will emerge in those industries. There are several other resources to monitor such information listed below.

It's one thing to understand and identify trends. It is another to realize a tangible opportunity and capitalize on it. Thus, if you see an opportunity in a growing niche position, industry, product, or process—engage it. It may take time for you to discover a niche within your field that will be right for you. You just have to keep your eyes open and be ready.

For example:

A financial planner who works with 401k retirement plans sees the rise in 529 college savings plans, and becomes an expert on it. He writes books, holds seminars, and even does TV interviews on the subject.

A veterinarian sees a study that pet lizards will boom over the next decade. She becomes one of few in the country to specialize in treating lizards. She creates a website called lizardvet.com sponsored by a pet food chain where consumers can order lizard food and medicine online.

An information technology professional capitalizes on the demand for bluetooth wireless technology, making that his area of training and expertise. He charges companies high consulting fees to plan and implement changes to their current IT infrastructure.

It's great to be aggressive and opportunistic, but also understand the potential downsides and consequences. Be cautious, and examine every opportunity closely. Many learned this lesson in the "dot.com" to "dot.bomb" period of the past decade. However, who knows…you just may end up on this fortunate *Fortune* magazine list:

"THE TEN RICHEST UNDER 40"

Michael Dell, 38	CEO, Dell	$17.1 billion
Pierre Omidyar, 36	Chairman, eBay	$7.1 billion
Jeff Bezos, 39	CEO, Amazon.com	$4.9 billion
Jeff Skoll, 38	Chairman, Skoll Foundation	$3.9 billion
David Filo, 37	Co-founder, Yahoo	$1.5 billion
Jerry Yang, 34	Co-founder, Yahoo	$1.3 billion
Sergey Brin, 30	Co-Founder, Google	$900 million
Larry Page, 30	Co-founder, Google	$900 million
Dan Snyder, 38	Owner, Washington Redskins	$740 million
Ken Griffin, 34	President, Citadel Investment	$725 million

(From the September 15, 2003, Issue of *Fortune*)

Similar to the astronomical odds of a 5-year-old basketball player actually reaching the NBA, the odds of making this list are equally against you. However, all of these people faced the same astronomical odds. Someone has to make it…why not you? When scrolling through this list, you can ask yourself what these people have in common, and are they really that different from you? Are they that much smarter or better than you? Probably not as much as you think. So why are they on this list? These people are risk-takers and go-getters, who seized an opportunity within their niche.

"Aim high, and shoot straight."

There is something to be gained from top entrepreneurs, entertainers, athletes, and even politicians. They all dreamed, and against tremendous odds, they succeeded. Famous sports promoter Don King wrote a book on his road to fame and fortune, aptly titled *"Only in America!"* He jumped from serving prison time for second-degree murder to becoming the wealthiest and most influential sports promoter of all time. Now, that isn't the career route I would recommend for you, but it is a lesson to be learned nonetheless. Oprah Winfrey is another tremendous example of opportunity in this country. Her achievements overcoming poverty and abuse in rural Mississippi are one of the most remarkable and inspiring stories in American history.

Not every college graduate enters the working world with the ambition and desire to become rich and famous. In fact, many people are content with a long career at the same job, with the same company. They may enjoy what they do, become routine-oriented, and reach a comfort level with their job. They may find that their job is easy, or becomes easy to them over time. Or, maybe they just don't want to be challenged.

However, at the end of their career, many of them might ask themselves *"What if?"* My advice is to not let too many *"What ifs"* pass you by in life. You can't control *"What ifs."* You can only control *"What can be."*

Think big, be unique, and try to seize opportunities by giving them your best shot. If you don't at first try, you will never achieve anything of any significance. Stay positive and believe in yourself. If you don't believe you can ever become that next star in your profession, believe me—you won't!

> *"Nothing happens unless first a dream."*
> -Carl Sandburg

I don't believe people entering the workforce after college dream enough. Instead, they get a job, start working at 8:00, and go home at 5:00. They become just another American employee, on the road to working 40 years, and then retiring. This is your life! Make something great out of it. You are young enough to be inspired, creative, and imaginative. You are also young enough that you have time to realize those dreams. Create your own dream and develop a plan to make your dream happen.

Recommended Books

Millennials Rising: The Next Great Generation
Neil Howe, William Strauss – Vintage, 2000

Go For It: Finding Your Own Frontier
Judith Kleinfeld – Epicenter Press, 2003

*TrendSmart: The Power to Know What's Coming...AND...
What's Here to Stay*
Louis Patler – SourceBooks, 2004

Good Luck: Creating the Conditions for Success in Life and Business
Alex Rovira, Fernando Trias de Bes
Wiley Business Trade Books, 2004

Occupational Outlook Handbook: 2004-2005
U.S. Department of Labor – JIST Publishing, 2004

Recommended Websites

www.life-after-college.com/articles
www.bls.gov/oco/oco2003.htm
www.trendwatching.com
www.shapingtomorrow.com
www.thinksmart.com
www.googlealert.com
www.wfs.org

Recommended Magazines

Fast Company   *Business 2.0*
Wired   *Harvard Business Review*
Technology Review   *The Futurist*

Create Your 5-Year Plan And Start Achieving It Today

Businesses have 5-year plans and 10-year plans. You should, too.

Hopefully, everyone who has taken business courses should understand a business plan. This is actually a novel concept. A business plan consists of financial goals, along with the objectives, strategies, and resources it takes to achieve those goals. Doesn't it make sense for people to do this as well?

One major impact I want this book to have is that college graduates need to focus on more than just the goal of "getting a job." Unfortunately, this is simply step one on your road to achieving happiness and success in your life and career. You need a plan. Where do you want to be and how exactly are you going to get there? The planning starts now, and the execution starts right after your planning is complete.

It is OK to have a financial goal. In fact, I encourage it. Certainly, I do want to reinforce the point that making a certain amount of money may not be everyone's goal, and may not bring you happiness. Nevertheless, let's say you want to make $100,000 within five years of college graduation. Is that physically possible to achieve? Research it and develop a plan. More than likely, the answer is "Yes."

Will it take two promotions, because you know that's what your boss's boss makes? Will it take a move into a different department, or a competitive company that pays more? Will it require a masters degree? Or, will it take doing something on the side, or starting your own company altogether? For that, you will first need to gain a tremendous amount of experience, resources, and capital. This will force you to create a plan.

Perhaps you find that the salespeople in your company make that amount, but it will be difficult for you to make that in five years at your current position. You may decide to develop your own skills in sales as you work and develop your knowledge in the field. Perhaps you find that a client of yours in a related industry makes that income, but you need to have technical knowledge first. This exercise will really make you examine how to get there, instead of just floating through life hoping to get raises and promotions whenever they arise.

Always continue to ask yourself:

"Where do I want to be by age 25, age 30…or age 40?"

You must always have tangible plans throughout your career. Effective goals must be realistic and attainable. Create mini-goals, or sub-goals, that lead to the ultimate goal, and check them off along the way. You must also hold yourself accountable. No one will be checking to see if you've done your homework. It takes an especially focused and disciplined person to continue to set goals to be completed "by May 31st of this year" for themselves. If you have a difficult time doing that, join with a friend who is also motivated and keep each other accountable. People also use this for such activities as dieting or working out. There is a reason for the "buddy system." It works.

Don't get sidetracked with your career. You and only you are in charge of where your future is headed. Get on your computer and physically create the resume you would love to have two years from now. Aim high. What do you really need to bolster your chances of a getting a promotion, raise, or your dream job? What would you really want to flaunt? Winning an award? Gaining an initial promotion? Earning an industry certification? Participating in a key professional organization? Completing additional training? Earning a graduate degree?

Save this resume and print it out. These are now your goals, and your "To-Do" list over the next two years. Now, go get them done. Each time you reach those objectives, re-create your ideal resume again—and never stop building on it until the day you retire.

The formula for success in your career includes many ingredients examined in this book. It includes hard work, time management, and striving to be the best at what you do. It includes being nice to people, being a good team player, and networking. It includes continuing to learn and develop as a professional in your field. It also includes doing the right things, and not doing the wrong things.

Most importantly, you must first determine what is important to you, and what will make you happy. Develop goals that align with what you value, and develop a plan to achieve those goals. Then execute the plan, and enjoy the rewards of your journey along the way.

Index

cubicle, 43, 54, 111
culture, 56, 77, 100
customer service, 46, 120, 135
customers, 64, 68, 69, 70, 83

D

dating, 102, 111, 112
Dederich, Charles, 21
degree(s), 20-23, 25-27, 41, 47, 138, 142, 147, 151
  B.A., 24, 58, 59, 129
  masters, 129, 130, 150
  M.B.A., 58, 59
  Ph.D., 129, 130
demand, 39, 40, 41, 48, 73, 74, 117, 118, 146
develop, 36, 41, 75, 76, 77, 90, 95, 101, 116,
  120, 122, 127, 136, 144, 148, 150, 151
diplomacy, 64, 103
discipline, 63, 89, 96, 97, 98, 103, 116, 129,
  130, 136, 151
diversity, 100
Dow Chemical, 89
dress for success, 37, 109-110
drugs, 91

E

EAP's, 91
Edward Jones, 77
e-mail(s), 20, 64, 70, 80, 82, 85, 88, 89, 90,
  102, 111, 125
embezzlement, 86
emotional intelligence (EQ), 100
emotion(s), 31, 64, 90, 100, 104, 111
employer(s), 26, 36, 37, 43, 44, 45, 48, 50,
  61, 64, 74, 86, 103, 121, 122
employment, 38, 39, 45, 49, 73, 91
Encyclopedia of Associations, 127
energy, 47, 57, 60, 64, 67, 95, 111, 116, 139
Enron, 86
enthusiasm, 58, 60, 67
entrepreneur(s), 140-142, 147
Entrepreneur, 89, 142
entry-level, 32, 61, 133
environments, 45, 55, 60, 61, 106, 135
Equal Opportunity Employment
  Commission (EEOC), 114
ergonomics, 54
ethics, 85-87
etiquette, 88-90, 106-108
expectations, 67, 79, 83, 95

experience, 21, 22, 23, 26, 27, 31, 32, 36, 41,
  46, 47, 48, 60, 64, 67, 72, 77, 102, 117,
  118, 130, 133, 140, 142, 150
experienced, 56, 78, 95, 103, 119
extra-curricular
  achievements, 48
  activities, 20, 46, 126
  clubs, 68
  concerns, 104

F

failure, 32, 82, 99, 123
family, 19, 26, 27, 29, 36, 44, 81, 104, 106, 116, 138
favor(s), 24, 58, 59, 76, 77, 78, 101, 113, 126
favoritism, 102
FedEx, 58-59
financial(s), 28, 34, 36, 40, 42, 73, 76, 77, 86,
  125, 130, 139, 142, 146, 150
fired, 59, 61, 89, 113
  termination, 97
first day, 21, 37, 53, 54, 55, 56, 58, 59, 80, 95
first job, 27, 35, 37, 47, 48, 49, 53, 56, 120, 122, 124
Forbes, 43
foreign (second) language, 20, 73
Forrester Research, 40
Fortune, 40, 77, 91, 147
fraud, 86, 87
friends, 19, 20, 25, 26, 27, 31, 32, 35, 43, 55, 61,
  76, 77, 86, 87, 89, 92, 99, 102, 112, 116, 128, 138
frustrated/frustration, 25, 55, 60, 82, 104, 121

G

global economy, 73
global market, 145
GMAT, 130
goal(s), 21, 32, 34, 67, 100, 109, 115, 116, 134, 150, 151
go-getter(s), 44, 61, 68, 76, 147
gossip, 60, 100, 111
government, 22, 24, 44, 146
graduate school, 129-130
GRE, 130

H

Hewlett-Packard, 45, 141
high school, 28, 103
hiring manager(s), 45, 46, 47, 78, 88, 97, 120, 123
hobbies, 29, 42, 75, 106, 116, 125
honest(y), 61, 71, 85-87
HotJobs.com, 49

www.life-after-college.com

Your home for life after college resources.

Order additional copies of **LIFE AFTER COLLEGE**
What to expect and how to succeed in your career

For **e-book download:**	www.life-after-college.com
To Order **via Internet:**	www.life-after-college.com
To Order **by E-mail:**	orders@life-after-college.com
To Order **by Phone:**	Call (888)674-7355 and have credit card ready
To Order **by Fax:**	Complete and fax this order form to (636)527-0977
To Order **by Mail:**	Complete and mail this order form with payment to:

Hawthorn Publishing, PO Box 1167
St. Louis, MO 63022-1167

Retail Price:	$14.95
Shipping:	$ 3.95 (within U.S. only)
Total:	$18.90

For orders within the state of Missouri:
Please add $0.91 for sales tax. If you are a MO reseller, please provide MO state resale number: _____

Quantity of Books: _____ (Only one shipping charge of $3.95 applies per order)

For information about discounts for orders of 20 or more,
call 1-888-674-7355 or e-mail orders@life-after-college.com.

Shipping Address:

Name: _____

Address: _____

City: _____

State: _____ Zip: _____

Phone: _____ E-mail: _____

University or Organization: _____

Please send check with payment, or complete credit card information below:

☐ Check   OR   ☐ VISA   ☐ MasterCard   ☐ AMEX   ☐ Discover

Card Number: _____ Exp Date: _____

Name on Card: _____

Signature: _____

Order should arrive within 5-7 business days upon receipt. Within 10 days of delivery, you may return new, unopened merchandise in its original condition for a full refund.

☐   **YES, send me a FREE DVD demo on Andy's *"Life After College™"* program for my University or Organization!**